On Our Way to Paradise
The Book of World Peace and Human Progress
Second Edition

The Practical Application of Human Values
Ideals and Goals Worth Having

Part 1 - Universal Core Values

Part 2 - Constructing a Society We Want to Live In

Part 3 - Tier Two Domestic Issues

2

Key Points in the Book

Philosophical Summary

Life on this planet presents a struggle to all humans
We must work together to make life better
The 'Common Benefit' is the cornerstone to an equitable society

Political Summary

Consumer and worker protections are essential
Jobs for everyone wanting to work
Living wages are essential, partial employee ownership is ideal
Caps on interest rates, medical and legal costs
The time has come for universal healthcare
There is no place for hunger, poverty, or war in the new world
We can structure a worldwide middle-class
Open communications between all citizens worldwide

Foreword

The Practical Application of Human Values

This book outlines political, cultural, and civic changes required to lessen the struggle humans face in living on this planet and to build a more equitable society.

For whatever beliefs we may hold there is a limited and basic set of universal human values that will enable people to work and live together. These common values can serve as a foundation that can be woven into a peaceful and progressive society without which there is too much chaos in our human interactions.

While much of this book is for American citizens, it is also written to and about people in distant lands who are beyond our eyesight but not beyond our ability to impact their lives. Removing people from lives of desperation, whether at home or abroad, is the number one way to replace destructive behavior with civilized behavior. It will lead to less armed conflict, less human violence, less crime and theft, and less misery among those who struggle to survive. It is also the right thing to do.

Some of the sections in this book address timeless issues while others address issues that have arisen in current events. Almost three decades ago I sat down at my office and wrote out the short essay that follows in which I listed my aspirations for a progressive society. Later, in 2008, with the election of the most liberal president in my lifetime, I thought my hopes had been answered but that has not been borne out in the way I imagined. There is still work to do in just about every field along with a need for a constant reinforcement of positive values if our society is to come closer to reflecting the ideals that we can imagine but find challenging to implement. Most of all, this book is not about some distant hope but for change now and today. As daunting as it might seem, it will never be easier to bring change than now and the people who are needed to bring the change will never be more prepared or able than the people of today. As the reader, you could very well be one of the people this book has in mind.

In general, most advanced countries have laws and cultures that are geared toward individual freedoms and there is little to structure people into united goals. While we want to retain individual freedoms we also want to lean toward more purposeful lives and goals where we assure all citizens some protection from the struggles of life and afford everyone the basics needed for survival. At the same time we want to diminish the effects of our negative traits such as the exploitation of others. We want to structure our governments so the leaders cannot strike out at others within society and beyond their borders to attain more wealth or power. Here are the original ideals I wrote about years ago and in this book I have added ideas, ideals, and proposals on how to get there and ways to pay for it:

Ideals and Goals Worth Having

In this new age of globalization, the world is connected by commerce, broadcast communications, and linked worldwide through the Internet. Distance no longer serves as a buffer to separate the great differences between the people of the world: differences in ideology, culture, and religion. As such, no country can isolate itself from problems around the globe.

Today, the world is too populated for any individual to live outside the realm of human society. Nor can any country isolate itself from problems around the globe. The poorest of people can see how the richest among us live and vice versa and the terror of war in one land can spill over to impact another or upset the world order. When war or economic strife afflicts one country, it easily affects the condition of those surrounding it, and even those across the globe.

Notwithstanding obstacles that are both real and imagined that divides the world's people, surely there are compelling universal social and cultural values that can foster harmony among the people of the world and foster a safer, saner, and more progressive world.

If human advancements are important to us, humanity needs a social system that puts those core values into a format that people from all over the globe can embrace regardless of nationality, culture, religious affiliations, etc. It is both plausible and essential that civilized people come together to promote the common interest of everyone to avoid catastrophic human or natural disasters by using all the resources at hand to speed-up and enhance human advancement.

Civility is a learned behavior brought on by the social environment in which we are raised. If society is to advance, end poverty, conquer war, or to make any pretense to seek a more enlightened society we must constantly reinforce civilized behavior. For civility to succeed at one hierarchical level of society, we must practice it at all levels.

It is time for our social and human advancements to keep pace with our technological advancements to make the world a better place to live. The industrial world is masterful at creating products and developing markets. It is with that intensity that we should apply our skills and our vast resources to address some of the world's most pressing problems as humans struggle to live on this planet. We should use all the resources available to make that happen in the atmosphere of limited government, limited taxes, and maximum personal freedoms.

This is a time to triumph over the chaos that divides us and bring civility to the world. That is a dream worth having for today's people.

To accomplish this goal there is a need for comprehensive and specific planning detailing what the problems are and how permanent solutions can be implemented. Then the requirements for implementing those solutions must be calculated using statistical and pragmatic approaches. It is not expected that we will have all the answers. But it is expected that we acknowledge the problems and set a specific course for their resolution. We can start by taking the first easy steps: collecting information, developing strategies, estimating requirements, and all things necessary in planning the advancement of a society.

It is not enough for developed countries to send armies to champion freedom across the globe. Freedom alone is not enough for the goal of civility to be reached. In addition we should make it our task to create stable environments among those that continually find themselves in dire living conditions.

Across the globe, many of the world's inhabitants suffer from curable diseases and 22,000 human beings die each day from starvation. An additional one billion of the earth's inhabitants go to bed undernourished each night. A good portion of the earth's citizens have inadequate shelter from the elements or no shelter at all and over one billion of this planet's workforce earn less than one dollar a day. Six billion humans on this planet own nothing more than the clothes on their backs. Meanwhile, the people of the developed world have the highest prosperity the world has ever known. It is both a humanitarian gesture and a pragmatic strategy to assist those who are living in human misery around the world.

Through our governments the world could take emergency steps to resolve hunger issues with temporary measures until permanent solutions can be planned and put into place. We should develop timetables: A timetable to end starvation; a timetable for the curing of diseases; etc. For example:

End starvation across the planet in five years
End war starting now
End all forms of poverty in twenty years
End all curable diseases in thirty years

Too many people around the globe suffer from diseases and illnesses that are easily treated with today's medicine. When the developed countries have such wealth and overall high standards of living, surely every person on the planet could have a basic health exam once a year or for the healthy once every three years. An active global society could have this in place in ten years.

Along with establishing timetables, we should work toward societal milestones. We need to work toward the first day when no person goes hungry in the world and the first day when no one in the world is killed in a war anywhere across the planet. We should work for the first day no one is murdered in any of our cities.

While there are many problems abroad, we have pressing problems here at home in the USA. We have significant poverty in our own country and for all our commercial successes we need social and cultural improvements. Many of our citizens' lives are stress-filled and too many are not finding economic and social well-being. Too often, we are all preyed upon by those who seek to exploit our human weaknesses for profit. At home, Healthcare is often available, but the costs are too high and while justice is available in this country, the system is too complex, too aloof, and too costly.

We cannot expect to raise our standard of living and our quality of living if we do not raise the consciousness of the people in our society. If advancements are desirable they must be planned for and expectations must be set. Through practicing civility ourselves and expecting it from others, we let it be known that there is a growing interest in making human advancements that are commensurate with our public abilities.

This is the type of world I wish to live in. These are the types of goals that befit a world that has attained our level of resources, knowledge, and abilities. I ask you to embrace, promote and develop them to turn all our good thoughts and heartfelt wishes into actions.

Jim Davis

Part 1 - Universal Core Values

Chapter 1 - Reality and the Material World

The primary reason for human organization is for the common, specific, and direct benefits it offers the individual, but it is difficult to view any social structure that does not have human advancement as one of its chief components.

A civilized society has the responsibility to provide peace, security, justice, and freedom so people may pursue individual tranquility and happiness. These things should be available to all the people in every country of the world. We need to foster these better aspects of our nature by promoting goodness, well-being, personal freedom, and harmony for the common benefit of the individual and common good of society. Given the world's vast resources, we have come upon a time in our history where every family in the world could and should have a shelter, have the basic elements to support life, and even the opportunity to enjoy living. In return for these social and economic assurances, people have a responsibility to live within a specific civil code and be productive citizens.

I propose positive changes in the financial and political systems where they are hindering society in America and globally. These changes in our societal structure can be obtained while providing reasonable levels of personal freedom for the individual. Nor is it required that the more successful and powerful elements among us who are amassing wealth be overburdened. In fact, that could be counterproductive. Many of the changes I propose make life easier for most of the wealthy too; but there are places where it is in all of society's interests to rein in business when the pursuit of profit begins to exploit or overburden workers, consumers, or the community at large.

We should be mindful that time passes quickly for each generation's chance to make their contribution. Because of an inventive few in each generation we have made great technological advances that should be translated into social advances if we are to change the world. Technical advances and commercial innovations are easy when compared to making social and cultural ones but history will judge us critically if we celebrate enriching the lives of the successful business elites if the masses are left behind. Because of our industrialism and technology we are now ready to go to this next level. The goal of this book is to bring enough people together to plan out a social and civil system where every human being on the planet is important in our civil and social system. This includes developing a complete system where each human being on the planet can have their basic needs met.

Chapter 2 - The Struggle for Existence

There is a gentle but constant struggle for existence on this planet. The pivotal fact is that humans are on this planet and alone in the known universe. Actually we live on only a sliver of this planet. The top and bottom of the planet are impractical to inhabit and just from a climate aspect alone it is a challenge to live on most of the rest of the planet. Within the areas that can support human life there are cold and warm seasons of varying degrees from which we must protect our bodies from the extreme temperatures that can end life and we take great measures to protect ourselves from the more moderate temperatures that are merely uncomfortable by comparison. For most regions there are only a few weeks of each spring and each fall of the year where temperatures are ideal for pleasant living without any aids.

Beyond climate concerns, any human, be they rich or poor, can contract an endless number of mild illnesses and a good number of serious ones that can cause suffering and death. Even mild afflictions are bothersome like allergies and sneezing that happen to millions of people each season from anything from droppings from trees to any assortment of weeds, bushes, and flowers. Many have allergic reactions to anything from a dusty house or if they eat even a small quantity of peanuts. Then there are illnesses and diseases that plague men, women, and children alike that are so serious and saddening it would be distracting to our topic to illuminate them here.

We also must ensure our drinking water does not contain any variety of natural or manufactured contaminants. Not known as a problem until recently, but the air contains a few natural and many manufactured pollutants that can shorten life.

That does not even consider the wide range of difficulties in our relations with other humans. There, too, are many direct and indirect dangers that are only lessened by humanity's willingness to organize and be civil toward each other.

Yet, despite all of this, humans inch ahead in terms of dominating the planet and overcoming the elements. Within the population people are working to make conditions better. There is also some wonderment of human life. There is the human spirit that motivates us onward with moments of joy and happiness between the struggles of life. Almost since the beginning of recorded history man has had the ability to imagine a more perfect world and express many forms of perfect and wonderful thought even while things around them were primitive. Slowly, life is getting statistically better for the human inhabitants.

Chapter 3 - Nature is Within Us and Society

Nature is full of competition for survival. The whole point of being human is to overcome that aspect of nature within us and to cooperate and work together for the common good within a group structure. We have those among us who say, 'let us compete among us for efficiency.' Then before we notice there are winners and losers; we have the 'haves' and the 'have-nots,' and we are back to nature. As we shall discuss, for group members to agree to cooperate we must all win enough to make staying in the group worthwhile.

In nature there are predators and prey as well as many species having a social hierarchy of alpha members and those who are lower in the social structure. Humans also have this trait in us as one of these hierarchical species. It is our learned environmental behavior that allows us to put aside this mentality and treat each other civilly. The pattern we have developed in our socialization is to reinforce the positive behaviors and strive to put aside the traits more often found in species that lack altruistic learning. In general, we seek to overcome our nature through learned civilized conduct. It is civility in the largest sense. Humans, with a higher degree of intelligence and communicative skills than most animals have the potential to create a world in which it is no longer focused only on merely surviving but on living life to the fullest potential.

In the course of human progress people have formed societal structures with civil, social, and moral codes and values. Putting aside the specifics and validity of any set of them, we do know that humans are not perfect and most of us fail to live up to all the standards we embrace all of the time. Hopefully, the rules that most of us have broken are smaller ones. I am not sure whether people are born as a clean slate and we are socialized with certain values or whether we are born with a genetic baseline of morality. After many decades of thought on this I am leaning more toward the notion that humans have an innate sense of right and wrong. In either case I think that in any given society there is a tendency for the civil, social, and moral codes to break down unless there are gentle reminders to reinforce good behavior. When we find values beneficial to the whole of a society it is incumbent upon us to gently promote them in a way that reinforces the values without being overbearing. Too much pressure will most often result in a backlash, just the opposite for what is wanted. There is an art to this whether one is talking about an individual or a nation. It is most often better to live by your values and presume that others see them and their merits, leading by good example. When that does not work, I do see it is difficult to stand by and watch an increase in negative behavior that will decay society.

One constant thread throughout human events is that people see things from their own perspective. In general, people bring to bear their own experiences. It is difficult to get more than a few people to see the same event and come away with the same judgment on what happened and what to do about it. If fifteen people meet to try and resolve an issue it is not surprising to end up with fifteen different views on how to address it. Even worse, people see all other views as unworkable. Even within a group of people with similar backgrounds, individuals can have different points of view of the same matter. It is impossible to enumerate all the various reasons for those differences. We just know it is often difficult to find agreement among people. It often comes down to what people see is in their best interests but deciphering how they perceive their best interests is hard to gauge.

Another problem is that people can be misunderstood when they try to communicate any number of things in language, mood, or actions. Humans are argumentative because they are sometimes selfish and sometimes because they honestly see the world differently. Some people are not as removed from instinctive behavior as others and all of us, I suspect, have moments when we act from emotion rather than from reason or intellect.

Another notable activity we want to highlight again is the human tendency to be the alpha member of the species. We may not hunt down wild boars for food any longer as our ancestors did thousands of years ago, but we take that inclination to hunt and the inclination to dominate into an entire range of activities from sports to seeing business competitors as prey and sometimes even our customers or people in our personal life.

It would have been the best arrangement if people could coexist with each other in general harmony without any problems and without any written rules and laws. People, one can imagine, should know how to get along with each other. However, that is not the reality. If we are to live in a free but orderly society in general harmony we will need not only have rules and codes, but we must root out the basic human defects that are the cause of violence, killing, aggression, and the human desire for dominance. They seem to go on despite having rules against them. We are still captive to primitive instincts from our warrior-conqueror-hunter past where the only rule was survival of the fittest. If modern society is to progress we must all have a common understanding of these base motivations that show up in everything from our daily interactions, business dealings, to our real reasons for going to war. Once we can expose these factors we are one step closer to living in a world governed and guided by reason. If we as individuals truly understand why we have such rules, restrictions, goals, and freedoms we will be more likely to go along with them, particularly if we see the overall package as beneficial to us personally.

Last, we can see uplifting themes in movies and can read them in books going back as far as the written word goes. Humans can express fine hopes but the reality has always been something less. Even when we have ideals we often cannot keep them. It seems there is a battle not only externally but internally as well. Whether we are fighting for resources or merely fighting for the attention of other humans we seem to run into conflict both individually as well as in any organization we establish. We wish for a world in which we live as one, but it is hard on most days to see how that will ever be a reality. While we seek peace individually and for society we must realize that as humans we have a built-in concern for ourselves. Probably some desires that pop up from time to time are like the desire for domination and other base things we bring with us from our past. But our self-interest is most often center stage.

Most of us have a workable set of ideals but have a hard time maintaining them. They defy consistency. For many of us our self-interest is still at the heart of our value set even when considering the world beyond us. We either have to base society on the survival of the fittest or recognize that what makes us valuable as humans is our ability to overcome our nature. That is what makes us worth saving as a species. We need to look out for ourselves while ensuring that others do not permanently fall behind the pack.

This does not mean we cannot trust our judgment or the judgment of others. However, it does provide us with a basic set of guidelines for human interactions that are composed when we are at our best and have a social structure that gently reinforces those values so they remain strongly held. As we learn to overcome our shortcomings or at least to live with them in balance, we need to expect our journey toward a better world to be an incremental one. People who care enough to read such books like this should not expect a swarm of instant and universal support among the wider public for higher consciousness. Indeed, they may not even be able to relate to such themes at all. A good portion of the public received their value set from traditional socialization in childhood and have had it ingrained within them before they are able to reason and decide values for themselves. For the population that never embraced critical thought or learning it is hard to introduce new themes into their life. Moreover, the further ideals drift from the perceived self-interest of people the fewer that will have an interest in supporting them.

Chapter 4 - A Universal Basis for Cooperation

If we feel that humanity is worth saving we must begin by reorganizing society so that all humans can feel life is worthwhile and that the societal structure they live in is valuable for them. It should not be just for the strong or the successful. It should not just be for those who have inherited wealth or abilities, nor for those who by accident of birth found themselves in a prosperous family or nation.

Humans tend to meander from one century to another with social progress primarily as a side effect of commercial advancements and new discoveries that can apply to human advancement in some way like medicine or efficiency in housing construction. Since the time of Homer the principles of human organization have been talked about but even today it is unclear to the average citizen as to the basic values in which society rests. Most of us spend a lifetime to gain the experience and knowledge we need to get through life and find ourselves unable to convey those values and lessons learned to our children or have that experience reflected in our governance, politics, or social codes. Today, we have groups among the public that advocate a political or religious set of beliefs and they actively work to force others to reflect the same beliefs through social, cultural, and civil laws. In America it has polarized many in the public and in some of the third world countries it is a source of conflict and violence. We must be able to express differing political and religious views while maintaining a basic set of more universal values that we adhere to when interacting within public arenas. Otherwise we will be locked into continual conflict and chaos.

There is a need for a basic set of universal, social, moral, and civil codes by which all people agree to live under in exchange for the developments and human progress they were born into and live among. This code is more basic and more limited than a full philosophy or a religion as it must span across many different people and different cultures. The basis of this code is that it is practical and sensible to live among people in cooperative efforts to lessen the struggle that life on this planet presents and it will afford people more freedom and opportunity for free pursuits than if they operate alone.

All people must benefit from the arrangement to make their participation worthwhile. Life must be satisfactory to each participant for this arrangement to be legitimate. The need for a code should be agreed upon, understood, enunciated, and learned by everyone in society. It is at least as important as the pledge of allegiance and certainly more universal as it applies to all people everywhere. It should apply to more than just one country and person but to everyone who wishes to interact with others. While some humans may become positive forces on their own it is in the best interests of the society to introduce and reinforce good values by educating people toward good behavior and reinforcing the desire for good behavior as all people can have moments of weakness.

True universal values are those that are adopted by the members freely as they understand they will benefit from them personally and that they are available and extended to all members. As a rule people do not accept a value with which they do not agree. They might nod in approval under force or pressure but only in free will is anything truly achieved. That does not mean you are free to adopt any value you happen to like. In a social structure a set of ideals must fit inside the overall values of the group to keep the society running and reduce conflicts and chaos.

One of the first values that people want is to have the freedom to do things in their self-interest, for their self-benefit, or for their pleasure. Obviously, it is not long before conflicting desires arise that need to be resolved. There must be a balance between an individual's interests and limitations placed by others in a group interest. People can engage in activities that do not bother others, even if the majority would not choose to do that particular behavior themselves. In a modern world we all need not conform to every set of preferences.

The Common Good

As early humans found, we can get more done as a group. Now, as then, to be in groups we must live within the code of the group. United, it is easier as we struggle against the challenges life presents on this planet. It is beneficial when people act in the public interest by doing something that moves society toward human progress and maintains or improves the human condition. When we work together for the common benefit of the complete community that is the 'common good.' The common good is one pillar of the universal set of human values.

Direct Benefit

While working towards the common good of society is likely to benefit an individual it, in itself, is not enough. Being a member of a society is some type of formal or informal social contract. If we are to freely join the group and live within its boundaries there must be a direct, individual, incentive for each member to do so. Further those direct benefits must be satisfactory and obtainable to that person or else they have less incentive to be productive and law-abiding members. There is no 'common good' if the individual members do not directly and individually benefit and see it as a beneficial and satisfactory arrangement.

It is not sufficient for 'opportunity' for success to be available as that is subjective. The individual must be satisfied with the conditions or else the whole of the group must investigate to see that opportunities are available and within reach of all members. Either way the group must aid that individual to see that they have as much success as possible as society cannot neglect any single individual to be legitimate.

Over time, we see activities that harm society or individuals within a society and we make forbiddances to those actions. We see that human violence harms others. We see robbing and stealing from others is hurtful and counterproductive to the furtherance of society. Tricking people from their earnings harm's society by misleading people. Therefore it is wrong in that it is harmful and counterproductive toward making life easier for humans. To lessen the burden on individuals, to maximize work and earnings and to further society we need only have a code based on things that offer a common direct benefit to the individuals that is within the common good and common benefits of the society as a whole.

Civility

Among the tasks of a civilized people is to eliminate human violence, remove people from lives of desperation, and reduce the human struggle. These are the basic obstacles that people face. The behaviors that contribute to human progress and facilitate human interactions make up the 'Standards of Civility.'

We rightly think of civility as being courteous and having a formality in greeting one another. Good manners are certainly intertwined with this full meaning of civility and are surface evidence that the bearer wishes for civility. Civility in this context is a standard of public conduct in all interactions and our steadfastness to the principles of the common good and the common (direct) benefit. It is more than politeness in meeting; it is an adherence to goodness in our relationships with others, in our business dealings, and all the way to include our nation's foreign policies. What it does not cover does not exist.

We should always gently reinforce positive values and we must provide reasonable safeguards to encourage people to refrain from bad behaviors like stealing and provide some reasonable penalties when they occur. Whether we are born as a blank slate or whether we are born with an inclination to certain values, we generally accept that society has a general moral and civil code that it feels will promote society's interests and values. At least it is hoped that the codes are agreed upon freely and have the general welfare of the whole group at its center.

An impediment to peace and harmony is that support diminishes as the list of values and virtues grow from the basic ones as people have differing viewpoints and perspectives. The base values must be not only fair, but kept short, simple, and precise so that everyone can remember them, support them, and keep them universal. Basic human values reflect civility: human progress, compassion, knowledge, reason, self-improvement, moderation, and reciprocity.

Also, in every aspect of principles I speak about is something so basic I rarely mention it as I take it as a given. That is, harming human beings is wrong and repugnant to progressive living. In our culture and most cultures, human violence is so commonplace it seems part of the fabric of living. This need not be the case and with a concerted effort humans harming other humans can become less frequent and perhaps one day something thought to be out of the bounds of a civil society.

Decadence

There are virtues we universally acknowledge as desirable and beneficial even if people do not live up to them every minute of every day. People have moods and it is too much to expect perfection from any human. On any given day, a person can say or do the wrong thing. Technically, every action takes us toward or away from goodness and the common good. It either benefits or advances a society or it does the opposite and takes us further away from these positive values and away from human progress. Sometimes people's actions, either wittingly or unwittingly, take us away from our positive values and goals. When people knowingly and continually take us away from our goals it decays society and that is decadent, bad, and wrong.

We should not look for perfection from people but we should, for example, expect people to not scheme to find the most efficient way to take people's money without giving anything of value back. We expect more from people than to exploit the need for income in a tight market by paying workers less than they would otherwise pay. Where we find people using exploitative practices we should apply social pressure and civil laws to force them to stop.

Morality

Purposely acting in the common benefit is moral and to act outside this principle by purposely undertaking activities against human progress and against the common benefit is immoral. It is 'good' when you do something that takes society toward human progress and improves the human condition. That is beneficial to society. Anything that takes an individual or society away from human progress or diminishes the human condition is bad. Likewise, to exploit others is immoral. I think we innately understand that lying, cheating, leveraging others, etc. is basically harming another human, which is not a moral thing to do. Being cruel is immoral. In practical terms all human violence is immoral as it harms other people and retards human progress.

There are hard questions about morality, for example, is it immoral to make someone unhappy? The answer is it depends. Sometimes parents make children unhappy by not allowing them to do things that parents see is not in their best interest. Of course, few of us would see that as immoral or even as bad. However, if you are being wicked and tormenting someone that certainly is a different scenario. Sometimes, depending on the degree of the activity, some things are just merely a bad thing to do and do not rise to the level of being pointed out as being immoral.

Another hard point is it immoral for the super-rich to live extravagantly while others around them live in poverty? I suspect there would be some debate on this point, but I think a super-rich person would be well aware of the needy and would hopefully feel innately some responsibility to help others as they have the capability to do so. Often they have a great capability of doing so without sacrifice as they have so much wealth. I would not be quick to condemn the wealthy as a class of people until it could be shown that few wealthy help others. I would suspect and hope that wealthy people do see a responsibility and help whenever they can to the degree they feel that they can. but in conclusion, I do not at this point feel it is immoral to be wealthy. I do feel, however, that in a successful society it is immoral to have those within society who do not have the basic needs and requirements to meet the struggle that life on this planet presents. In short, it is immoral to allow suffering in a society that has the ability to prevent it. That should weigh heavily upon all of us, particularly the wealthy who are most able to do something about it.

Innate Morality

Something I stumbled on several years ago was the concept that people innately know right from wrong. It seems so basic, maybe everyone knew about it but me. Is it that humans have certain basic innate inclinations that are universal? I am thinking it is so more and more. Within this innateness we consider that 'we' automatically know that we should not harm other humans, at least without good cause such as in defense, we should not be violent toward others, we should not steal or oppress others. We should automatically know we do wrong if we wish to have dominion over another human. Harming or exploiting others is certainly wrong as is lying and deceit. This is by no means a complete list but it would be a good start if we started living within the bounds of what people know innately to be right. I think many of us do this daily. Not because we have learned in school, from our elders, or from a set of laws, that some behaviors are wrong but because we already know it to be wrong.

An Obligation to Help Others

There are good reasons why we should help people help themselves. Beyond the humanitarian aspect there is also a more basic principle to consider. When people are members of society they expect to have some benefit from their participation. There are a good number of people in society (at home and abroad) who are not really benefiting from the societal structure. Successful members may claim disaffected members need only apply themselves by pulling themselves up by their shoelaces. Until then many are content to leave them on their own until they submit to starting at the lowest rungs and be content to work their way up. However, that method has been unsuccessful. Maybe the road is just too long or maybe there are not enough opportunities.

Society has an obligation to help all its members' progress because all the members are participating by being civil and by going by the rules. Otherwise there will be less of an obligation from the members who are not benefiting from societal rules to go along with them. An increase in crime is one likely result. Each time a society sees a large segment of its membership is failing then adjustments are needed to have more people in successful scenarios. Likewise, if a segment of society forms policies and rules that diminish and fragment the society, the society must step in and correct the rules to ensure that most people have a reasonable chance to be successful. We are obligated to help those who struggle even when they are the ones that are the most difficult to help.

It is my observation that in many decades of living I have found a sense of happiness can come from helping others. When a person helps others and when they are around people who they care about as much as they care about themselves it produces a source of contentment with life.

Whatever our mindset, we must examine our place in the universe long enough to realize we must help each other and that it is to our own benefit to do so. In the modern world we must integrate our desire to have a better life for ourselves, our family, and loved ones with the notion that we are all connected and adapt to a purpose driven life and be part of a purpose driven society. Through this individual will find more peace and progress and so will the society around them if it is done on a broad basis to include all of humanity. We must not only require that our governments leave out war but we must also implore our neighbors not to exploit others in business and in personal dealings. It is no more simple or complicated than asking to treat each other as we would wish to be treated, a three-thousand-year-old sentiment.

Gentle Temperament

Few of us are always of gentle temperament but that is when we are at our best. When we are either anxious or agitated we might not be our best version of ourselves. Only the lucky few are free from some degree of mood changes and we need to see that in ourselves and learn to not only notice it, but control moods that would hinder us in our outlook on life, our judgments and particularly dealings with others. Ideally, I think, we want to speak with a gentle voice both to others and to ourselves. In my view, when we get away from our better self when we are pushed by the natural instincts within us toward emotionally mixed judgments and away from intellectually based behavior. This in no way means we should fight feelings of all emotions, but it does mean we should hesitate to feed into aggression and anger in social situations and all areas where we are not being physically attacked.

Many of us cannot tell the difference between a comment, criticism, and a physical attack. There are people that have an ever-increasing list of triggers that result in conflict. Society would benefit from increasing the importance of civility in public and the gentility inside us to promote harmony within us and among us. If recent history has taught us nothing else it has taught us that once public figures do not keep the discussion between the lines of civility that those on the fringe will carry it even further and from civility to violence.

The Pursuit of Happiness

The American constitution states that individuals in America must have the right and ability to pursue happiness. "Life, liberty and the pursuit of happiness" are given as examples of "unalienable rights." It states that it is given to all humans and that governments are created to protect those rights. The most fundamental legal document in America requires all of us to set up a social and legal system where people have the opportunity to be happy. Primarily that would mean free from oppression and free from being overburdened. Not only should the laws not be oppressive but all aspects of society not be oppressive. This is important in advocating fundamental changes and in commercial societies like America, it means changes in commerce.

Purposeful Lives

It need not be so complicated. We merely need a social code that is based on the common good and direct benefit where everyone benefits from the structure, that it helps all and harms none. A citizen deciding to be a member of a society asks, "What is in it for me and what is expected of me?" So any society had better offer benefits to the individuals within the group and it must also protect the individual from unjust harm from the group or powerful individuals and institutions within the group. It is the basic concept of having majority rule with minority rights. Today, no one should settle for being left out in the cold and as a species we can do better than what we are doing now.

If we do nothing else we have, here in this book, outlined a workable set of universally acceptable basic values that would allow all of us to reach for peace and human progress. With these fundamental human and innate values I am advocating in this book is that we all sit down and design a world that we would like to live in. Let us start fresh. We can't build a better world if we don't first know what we would like it to look like. We would want a simple and positive foundation that can be universally embraced like the common good, a common direct benefit, and civility. We would want a world in which all people are offered some aid as needed to protect us all from the struggle this planet presents and protection from the harshness of hunger, poverty, and human violence. We would want all people in the world to have the opportunity to live a middle-class existence and have free time to enjoy their own pursuits. These are the kinds of things that are worth talking about and working toward. We may not achieve them easily or even agree on how to achieve them but we must start somewhere and this is the time to redirect our society, and the world, toward more purposeful interests.

Gentle Promotion of Goodness

Because of human weaknesses, failings, ignorance, and chaos there is a constant battle to maintain and promote 'goodness.' Additionally, people often revolt against restrictions and rules. Sometimes they don't even know them or recognize how they apply to their benefit. Rules, codes, and guidelines all need to be ones that people can see are helpful, useful, and beneficial to them directly. They need to see the rules as tools to advance society and human progress and see that such a path helps everyone, including them. Once established they should be gently echoed from time to time so that people remember them and recall how they apply to the betterment of themselves and the society as a whole.

Religion

While people hold to religious beliefs and philosophical values there is little agreement and insufficient flexibility in those approaches to build a universal society. Some countries have a state religion but it comes at the cost of freedom of expression and that has not proven to be a formula for a successful society. One of several problems with religious morality is that there are over 10,000 different religions in the world, many conflicting with each other in some regard or another. All claim they are right and all other religions are wrong. About 20 percent of the population does not hold to any religion. Additionally, religion simply covers too much. It goes too far into personal habits to serve as a universal foundation for human organization. While many pursue perfection within a religion or a philosophy the organization of the society must be guided by the minimum number of constraints and hinderances while offering universal protections and opportunities so people can rise above the struggle and obtain the basic comforts for living.

Part 2 - Constructing A Society We Want to Live In

Chapter 5 - Middle Class Ideals

The purpose of a 'world peace and human progress' organizational system is to reduce human struggle and promote human progress. As a group worldwide, we would work toward all people having the essentials of life and we want to move all people toward middle class living. For example, in a country as rich as America there is no reason we cannot have a social, civil, and economic structure that enables all Americans to prosper. People will have different levels of motivation and abilities but in America people who work and spend earnestly should be able to afford a nice home and be able to provide for their family needs. They should be able to obtain cars that are modern, efficient, and low maintenance. They want to have some money put away for an emergency and for any unexpected expenses. They would also like to still be able to afford at least one good vacation each year with a smaller one along the way with enough disposable income to pursue their interests and go out in the evening occasionally. Those are somewhat modest levels of living in the modern world.

Today, we are moving away from that economic model. This country used to have a national routine where people primarily worked during the day, during the week, and most all the factory workers were off on Saturday and hardly anything was open on Sunday. We used to have the forty-hour work week as the standard. Anything over forty hours was paid at time and a half pay. Today, we have jobs where ordinary people are paid a salary and they can work for sixty hours a week if the pay does not fall below the minimum wage for forty hours of work. If a person is making the national average salary they are not going to drop below that minimum wage so they can be on call for work any night or day at the same salary. That would not have happened in the old days. In recent years some minimal limitations have been placed on this but as of 2024 workers across America work overtime without being paid anything extra.

For a time college seemed to be a way of ensuring a good income but that is less true today. Also, working harder and longer to get ahead by itself will not assure people today of upward mobility nor can they expect the next generation to have it better than the last unless we make some societal changes. The hallmark of the American dream is no longer happening in great numbers. A recent study indicates that there is more upward mobility in Europe and some developing countries than in America. The list of countries that are ahead of us in this area is discouraging.

People need to have enough money saved away for a crisis or for times when fuel costs rise or utility costs spike and so on. That has not been possible for many working people lately. Middle and working class people have suffered through stale earnings while prices have gone up over time.

Unlike the financial and professional classes the working-class people have less time and ability to enter the political discussion and political decision-making process. They do not make enough money to afford to make political contributions to campaigns. Not only do they work but have the normal activities they more often must work on their own car, maintain their own homes, and so on and that takes the remainder of their time and energy. And lastly, they just do not have a pattern or history of participating in politics in large numbers unless they do so indirectly as part of a union or something similar.

Elections seem to be decided by those who can run the most media advertisements. This requires a lot of money and that is most available from the organized (special) interests. For the single reason of large campaign contributions from those with special interest, ordinary people citizens have little influence with public officials in Washington and at state houses. The unions are no longer strong enough to represent workers and the political parties have not done anything beyond campaign promises. Big businesses seek to lower wages and they are continually refining ways to extract the maximum amount of money from the consumer with the minimum responsibility for the usefulness or quality of the products they sell.

<u>Having disposable income is a requirement.</u> The machinery of free enterprise, if left unchecked and unbalanced, will evolve to where the worker makes only enough to survive while those who provide the capital manipulate the economic system.

In practice the worker and consumer have one only real voice in shaping the laws and that golden time is on election day. Unless we are going to have a country of haves and have-nots we will have to require the government to maintain a level playing field. This can be done and it doesn't take every citizen to get involved. The fact is that you are not going to get everyone to help, even when it is in their interests. A group of as little as thirty people can have an impact if they are addressing real problems and their message rings true in the community.

It is not that we need less government or more government, we need better government. The government is supposed to be reflective of the wishes of the public. If you think that the government has been taken over by special interests, then that is an important issue to address and correct. The government will serve those that get the candidates elected. If the special interests have too much influence it is because the ordinary voters need to speak up and be heard. Ordinary voters need more education at election time about the issues that are at stake. Often special interests cloud the election season with distractions, play on the fears of the voters, or stir up old prejudices from the past.

America now has a population of over 330 million people that are all born into a set structure that is based on free enterprise. There has always been a balance between the interests of business and the interests of rank-and-file citizens. My contention is that, today, the government looks too much toward business first and puts the people second. This is not that unnatural as business can afford to organize and has a financial reason to do so. They have lobbyists who have input into every law the government makes. Average citizens have no such lobbying group other than the elected officials themselves. That has not proven to be sufficient.

It is good to get a daily report of the stock market on the nightly news but the world should not revolve around Wall Street. It is the status of Main Street that must become the daily focus of the American consciousness. It will be tough to accomplish change with Wall Street claiming anything that does not give them a free hand will hurt the economy. Unlike the old adage about General Motors, what is good for Wall Street is not necessarily good for America.

In the richest and most advanced country in the world we should have no underclass at all. The poor and the struggling have, as a group, abided by the rules of society so within those rules must be measures to assist them to be more successful or provide the basic means for survival until they are self-sufficient. We cannot justify having a system where everyone must fend for themselves and still require those failing to sit quietly while the remainder of society makes progress. The growing underclass of citizens that do not benefit from the system is unreasonable and it only exists as there is not a set formula for changing it. The fact is we live in a system that we would not design for ourselves if we were starting over today.

The American Standard

We were once referred to as the 'can do' Americans. Americans should have high standards and there is no reason why Americans should be second to none in the quality of life. Americans should not accept anything short of having the highest wages of any workers in the world. It is baffling why we are ready to accept paying more for healthcare and more for prescriptions than everyone else in the modern world, sometimes twice as much as others. As Americans, we should strive to have the lowest cost university education, the most access to learning, and it should be easier for our citizens to seek justice than anywhere else in the world. We should have fewer poor, less discrimination, more programs to give the struggling a hand up. Many Europeans have a four months' vacation, but that is not the standard in America. Americans should have the lowest taxes for the number of services provided and offer the best goods and services at the lowest price and at the highest value.

Democracy Works Best with Managed Capitalism

In wanting political change or cultural change one must argue for it in open debate. Of course we all recognize coercion and oppression when we see it and few would want to maintain the rules of society by those means. When we see that happening around the world we conclude the people have too little invested in society or that they are not rewarded enough to be nonviolent and orderly so they are put into submission by force. Another characteristic is that some populations do not have the education to see how systems work and how they fit into it. But there must be a vehicle for not only communication with the government but the ability to impact the rules that citizens are obligated to live under.

In America we have a system of democracy although it is being bound more and more with the special interest as they refine their methods of manipulating government while the rank-and-file populations are not looking. The fact is ordinary people have rarely gotten involved in the running of their government and that is still true today. However flawed it may be, democracy has been the organizational vehicle that has led America to the top of the world in many categories. It is fair to say that the top rating is dependent on how one measures success and as we all know today America is not the leader in all areas and that is increasingly true in areas that are important to rank-and-file citizens.

The partner in American democracy is free enterprise and there is a constant pull one way and then the other on how raw our free enterprise system should be or how many protections it should offer to its citizens. I am in the category of wanting more protection for the rank-and-file workers and consumers of today. For decades we were told the middle class would be shrinking and that more of the wealth of this country would be moving to the top. There is no surprise that the trend is in that direction.

Chapter 6 - Unfettered Free Enterprise

Over the years, merchants have honed their craft and found more efficient ways to make money. There are several sectors of the economy that have developed into monoliths over the years and it has buffered them from free market forces. They use their size to dictate to an unorganized public who are almost powerless consumers. They use their size to influence laws through lobbying elected officials and they use their size to dominate commerce. All these things have added to the problems of a struggling middle class and the poor. What is important is the real buying power. Always compare the cost of goods against the income of consumers. Dollar amounts are relative. Incomes have gone up but not as much as expenses.

Years ago, the cost of items dropped when we began buying goods that were made overseas at one tenth the labor cost, but it was about half the quality. But the full benefit of that labor saving was not passed down, they were taken as profits by investors who wanted to make more money by shifting labor overseas. It saved customers some and it made investors more money. However, it cost American jobs. Instead of working in the mills and factories of America now that work force has shifted to retail stores and as waiters and waitresses. Workers are making less money.

We know living costs have inched up over the years while salaries have remained stagnant. Some workers have not had any wage increases in ten years, while the cost of the items they buy has doubled. If you look at the American economic system you will see that the financial class is doing well. Those are people who make most of their money from financial investments ranging from stocks and Wall Street activities to local investments in banks, businesses, and real estate. The problem is that over time they have taken over the free-market system and organized it so that if they make money they prosper and when they do not make money tax breaks soften their losses or perhaps enable them to defer the losses against other tax liabilities. Apparently if they fail in large enough numbers they can go to congress and get a bail out.

Companies who operate in the free enterprise system are constructed to extract as much money from the consumer as possible. They will extract all they can right up to where one more penny would cause the consumer to not buy or to buy from someone else. The threat of another company coming in and competing with their product or service is the competition that is supposed to keep prices in check. Over time, the theory goes, the market will arrive at the lowest price possible. But in today's world where companies are so big and products are launched on such a large scale it would take another large-scale company to compete with them. Those companies have been able to dominate the market without sufficient competition to bring prices down or keep quality up.

Consumers faced price increases in basic goods in 2022, 2023, and 2024. There is speculation that the increases in staple items were driven by a desire by dominant manufacturers and providers to take increased profits. It was not because they had higher costs in production and delivery. Most large corporations did record windfall profits over this period. This may be legal and within the principle of free enterprise but it is not demonstrating the social responsibility we will need from corporations as we go forward.

The Material World

It is hard to avoid the financial pitfalls of living in America. Today the products and services available in America are so tantalizing that most everyone is up to their neck in debt. Most of us work every day to make ends meet no matter what class of people we are or how good we live. We seem to be a society that wants to have material things and we want about as much as we earn, often more. If we earn more, then we want more. We use financing to get them now rather than saving our money and purchasing it outright. We pay interest to lenders for this privilege and by doing this it makes expensive things more readily affordable, but it enables the vendors to raise prices as they know that consumers can pay for items in installments. Items are not priced on a cost-plus basis, but on the free market principle of how much you are willing and able to pay for it.

Perhaps we need less commercialism in our society and more emphasis on people. We enjoy the progress our system has brought us, but it has taken some of the enjoyment out of living also. Life is always a struggle. The struggle for the poor is obvious as they cannot meet their basic needs and if they do one misstep will put them behind. The upper classes have a buffer from the harshness of life but much of the upper class is not that much further removed from the stress of commercial life in America. They have country club dues, yacht club dues, and their children attend private schools. Their bills add up just like ours. They have larger homes and therefore larger mortgages and so on. It seems like we have formed a society in which we are all constantly under stress to make money and pay bills. I know a family that has several good income earners and they have about two million dollars in the bank and convertible assets over one million dollars. Yet they worry about the money running out all the time.

We don't feel sorry for them because we see things they could give up and keep living. When many of these people are talking about smaller governments and less taxes they say it is because they pay a lot in taxes. However they do look for every way to make money and in the nature of things they see higher wages as another impediment to their goals. The workers and the capitalist are at odds in this area. Everyone is under stress in a free economy as it is constantly offering the raw cutthroat instability of competition.

It seems to me that we all have an interest in keeping the economy in balance. Even when the market shifts upward it hurts those who lost in the shift when it goes up and it eventually must come down. It would seem slow steady incremental growth would be the most stable, perhaps in proportion to the increase in population. Every time the economy tightens, most financial people are willing to throw everyone else under the bus. The free-market system is along the same principles as survival of the fittest. Not that admirable really. It seems the course would be to put in place safeguards to prevent the self-interest of the more able among us from overrunning the struggling people who are trying to get ahead themselves. We need merely develop a system where opportunities are abundant and safeguards are in place.

Chapter 7 - Capitol and Labor

Unions

Unions used to be a big factor in the American economy and American life. Unions were everywhere with about one and three workers belonging to some sort of union although fewer in the south than in the north. Today, you have to go back about 100 years to see a lower percentage of union labor, just before the great depression.

In the old days, a person would get a job in the manufacturing plant and when a new job came open workers would bid on it for seniority. Wages were negotiated by the unions. Worker protection was given by the company but the unions were the ones who stood up for you if there was a problem. It seemed to work. A worker could work at one company their entire life. Today that is no longer the case.

The world today is much rawer. Management has all the controls. Few worker protections are in place. One can be required to work without a break. One can be fired without cause. A person can be fired for just telling others what they are paid. There is neither seniority nor any pay scale system. In fact, there is not really overtime pay for non-management salaried employees. In Georgia you can work at a company for ten years and get laid off or fired without any notice or reason. Everyone expects to go from job to job and few expect to live in the same town as they change from job to job.

Although the standard of living of the workers seemed to be better when unions represented the labor force and the communities seemed to be more vibrant, it became popular to complain about unions and how they ruined this country. Neither workers nor unions were very effective at dissuading the public from those complaints about the $40.00 per hour auto worker. Then there is the talk about worker pensions. Little is said that most of the money from pensions go to cover the medical insurance and actual medical costs. To me that is a medical industry problem not a union-worker problem.

When a group of mill workers want to organize to demand fairness in a living wage it is socialist, non-competitive, and is anti-liberty. While people complain about organized labor do not forget that the doctors, lawyers, pharmaceuticals, and most big businesses are organized, too. They have paid representatives at every state house in the country and have paid lobbyists in the nation's capital, not for the general benefit of humanity but to look after their interests. Lobbyists cost consumers more than unions ever did.

What is it when pharmaceutical companies go to congress and convince them to make laws preventing governmental agencies from bargaining over the price of prescription drugs? The answer is twenty billion dollars. That is how much it costs the taxpayer each year according to a national group who studies medicine. It is only in 2022 that congress has passed a law to allow the government to negotiate drug costs with pharmaceutical companies. After decades of struggle it is only a partial victory and we will have to see how much it benefits the consumer.

Some like to say that the union workers were being paid beyond the merits of their work. They felt there is nothing special about repetitive labor so why pay so much for it. What critics do not consider is that line workers need to show up every day, no matter if something interesting is going on elsewhere or not. Workers say that they cannot even look away from the job for long and must focus on the job at hand for eight hours every day. A bathroom break needs to be scheduled as someone must take over that task on the assembly line. Small business owners like me and all the many small businesspeople that make up the conservative chorus in America would probably not be able to work under those conditions. As a business owner, I worked hard in my days at the office but if I ever needed to take a morning off I could. Line workers do not have that luxury.

Globalization

Unions did not hasten the decline of manufacturing in the US; it was globalization in a move toward cheap labor. There is such a disparity between the living standards of American workers and overseas workers that manufacturers can get workers for about $68.00 a month in countries like Bangladesh. The rising countries are making improvements in their wages. In Mexico and China the wage scale is now around $3 to $4 per hour (2022). These are the stated rates of pay by law but sometimes workers are paid less.

In the 1990's, Ross Perot, argued that NAFTA would cause manufacturing in this country to move their operations to Mexico and we would be able to hear a giant sucking sound as they moved. The government claims that NAFTA was good for America and that it has increased trade but the figures they offered included such 'exports' as crude oil which skewed the figures. Another key item is auto parts, which are not so much replacement parts for their cars, but for car parts for the vehicles they are assembling in Canada and Mexico that were once built in America. It sent the automobile and textiles jobs to Mexico. It also has the effect of freezing wages in America as labor had to compete with Mexican wages. Mexicans have a lower standard of living and they do not have labor rights, worker safety, or health benefits. About a third of the entire Mexican worker force is the result of NAFTA. The two largest plants in my rural town have closed. The other textile mills in the area closed too. The North Carolina furniture market has declined considering competition from China, Italy, and Mexico. While Mexico does not make up a large part of the furniture market it still accounts for about a tenth of the import total. The later version of NAFTA does little to change all that. It does help lower the cost of medicine going from the US to Mexico, but we still do not have the agreement we need which is an agreement that helps all workers in all countries.

A Seal of Approval

Still America, as the largest consumer, must ensure every item that is bought and every service is done by workers making a living wage. This could be done through formal legal means or through pressure applied by the consumers. If it does not have a seal of approval where the workers who made this product were paid a living wage, the environment in which they worked was tolerable, and that all was being done to minimally impact the planet, we should not buy it.

Break Up the Monopolies

When I was in school one of the simple principles we learned is that the government would step in a stop the formation of monopolies. I remember specifically studying case law where the government came in to stop companies from going into a market and under selling a product to get market share. Later, if unchecked, they would become dominant in that marketplace and they would go up on the prices to a level higher than they were before they started. Imagine my surprise when one of the first companies I worked for after college was underselling 'loss leaders' to attract buyers into their stores. Today there has been a great consolidation of companies into a comparably few corporations having major market share in many market segments. It is time to break them all up and require partial employee ownership of all corporations. The idea behind all of societies efforts at commerce is to reduce the struggle for all citizens not to make a minority of citizens wealthy. It is not a case of jealousy over the financial elite's great wealth it is that corporations have the narrow goal to make profits whereas today we need a more socially responsive commercial environment as the world transitions toward putting the emphasis on meeting the needs of all its citizens.

A New Department of Commerce

Today the Department of Commerce is charged with facilitating commerce in the United States and beyond. To the charter of the department we should require that it assure fair pricing, apply a quality rating, and rank customer satisfaction for all goods and services in the Unites States. The department should have a very comprehensive consumer support system and have a place on the internet that lists complaints and to follow up on them to see if the providers of goods and services have conducted business in a socially responsible fashion. It will be the ultimate customer complaint department.

This would be true of all medical services, legal services, automobiles sales and repairs, and all food sales and services. When a person goes to the doctor, for example, they would know what the initial visit would cost along with the cost of all the services that the office provides. They would also have access to a customer (patient) rating and other pertinent data. This would be true for all businesses providing goods and services in America. It would also cover all goods and services imported from overseas.

A primary plus is that all goods and services, including medical services, will have a price range along with the specific price a given doctor's office or medical facility charges for a procedure. That price will have to fall within that price range. If it is higher than the low range an explanation will be legally required from the provider and they simply are not allowed to charge outside that range. That will be true of all other goods and services too, including auto repairs shops. Some states require some of this now, we will be making it more comprehensive and more uniform in its application.

Worker Income

Today a worker makes much less than his counterpart in the 1950's and 1960's when looking at buying power and cost of living. The distance between incomes at the top and the bottom in this country continues to separate. Last year a leading stock investor made about $25,000 per minute while many American workers are stuck in jobs that do not pay that much in an entire year. Hard work has less merit when the payoff is a lifetime of debt and stress.

Wages are so low in some sectors of the economy that large retailers pay workers so little that employees are still eligible for welfare and food stamps. This is nothing more than the government subsidizing those companies. A sad fact since one of them, Wal-Mart, has put more small retailers out of business than any company in American history which was the plan of the founder.

It is surprising that women are still paid 25 percent less on average than men doing the same work in modern America. About one out of three women in this country live in poverty. Paying them the same as men for the same work would cut the poverty rate in half. That sounds like a simple and equitable solution. There was a bill in congress to provide equal pay for equal work but it was held up by the usual suspects.

The financial markets and the medical industries have been the top sources of income in America and the service businesses have done well too. However, the manufacturing segment is just too large to give up. America needs to add value to products to have the built-in profits to pay workers good wages. So many of our young people are so accustomed to seeing 'Made in China' stamped on almost all consumer goods and seeing foreign cars or American cars made with foreign parts, it is hard to remember we were once the leader in manufacturing. While the conventional wisdom was once that the American worker could not compete with the low cost of overseas labor, all is not lost. It is not that black and white. We can begin to recapture some of America's prior place in manufacturing, but the key selling points would be in making quality products. That is what we did in the 1950's. American products were always more expensive and worth it. That does not necessarily mean ornate or deluxe just making things that are practical, sturdy, and work as they should. There should be a seal of approval on every product made in America that meets quality and precision standards.

A New Department of Labor

Rather than have individual unions across the country, it is plausible that the federal government could expand the Department of Labor to include worker protections. This way all workers would have an agency that would be responsible for assuring all workers have job satisfaction and job security. The department could establish a fair wage scale, safe working conditions, and require a pleasant work environment. Think of it as a more socially responsible version of the free enterprise system we have now. We must move into a more balanced economic system or else a small percentage of the citizenry will have most of the wealth and that is not good for the society as a whole.

We should require the same working conditions and benefits that we would want if we were in their jobs. Good paying jobs create stability within a company that will result in better products and fewer problems for the company as would partial employee ownership if people will just try it.

The Formation of Work Partnerships

As a society we should move away from a work structure that puts one class of people in a position to have the financial incentive to keep another class of citizens down. We want to remove the situation where management is always asking labor to do more for less. The old 'employee' model is over. You can see that in the turbulence of today's workplace. I suggest a set of new business formation options that change the relationship between owners, management, and labor to bring them closer together and give more incentive to workers to consider the welfare of the company while working to earn money.

In this new system, capital provides everything but the labor and the two groups would split the profits on a percentage basis. This will also help with employee retention. In the new world workers are paid well and have a ownership share of the company they work for. In addition to fairness, it would give owners and managers some incentive to treat workers well and it would be an inventive way to make a better workplace environment.

For corporations in interstate commerce, the employees would receive a living wage according to an established wage scale and in addition to that they would receive a percentage of the company profits. For the largest of those corporations with more than fifty employees, half of the profits would be evenly divided among the employees. Within this amount would include receiving a living wage according to the jobs they are doing. In the end the capital and labor would roughly split profits on about a fifty-fifty basis. This may sound like shocking news to some readers but there have been calls for all corporations to be totally employee owned or community owned. I think this is a good compromise, particularly in America with its capitalistic system and managed economy.

Additionally, executives within those companies that seek to make more than ten times the pay of any worker would be taxed at a higher rate.

Invigorating Local Communities Everywhere

In the old days there were just a few national corporations like Sears and Roebuck and JC Penney. Those two alone were not significant enough to drain a local economy. However today the economic landscape has turned into mostly national chain stores and restaurants in most of the communities in America. Now an overwhelming percentage of the store's profits are leaving the towns of America going to Wall Street and other points north. This all must be reversed.

When we require large multinational corporations to structure themselves for partial employee ownership it changes to flow of their profits. Under this plan half of all chain store's profits will stay local. As a federal law it would apply to all stores that participate in interstate commerce, all companies with over fifty employees, and all companies with more than one location. This will help revitalize communities everywhere..

Minimum Wage

Congress has not addressed the minimum wage since 2008. It is simply hard to do in a political climate. If congress wanted to get away from the dollar figure and not have to revisit the issue each time the economy changes, they could index the minimum wage by requiring it to be at least three times the poverty level.

There are benefits to this arrangement. When everyone makes a living income there will be less need for government assistance. There will be less need for short term credit needed in daily living. People will be able to afford houses without 'maxing' out their ability to make the payments and they will still be able to afford some of their wants and needs. Plus, it will be removing people from lives of desperation which cause an assortment of social ills.

Worldwide Living Wages

This could be expanded worldwide by Americans as we are the largest consumer market in the world. Through formal legislation or public pressure we should require all products and services sold in America to be made by workers receiving a living wage of at least three times the poverty level for the region where it is produced anywhere in the world. This new partnership would balance the worker-employer arrangement worldwide.

Having overseas workers receiving a living wage will have benefits worldwide. They will then be able to purchase more things themselves and the consumer cycle will start all over again in developing countries. Having fewer struggling citizens overseas and fewer living lives of desperation will result in fewer people taking part in activities that have a negative societal impact. When an importer has not complied with this standard those items or services are not allowed into the country or is charged a fee that would equal twice the amount of the proper wage. Additionally, workers should also share in the profits just as in America.

Employee Pay Scale

All of us who grew up in a workshop are familiar with the old labor rate book that would tell mechanics (and customers) how much time a given repair should take. You simply took the parts cost and added the given labor time to any repair bill. Sometimes a mechanic could beat the given time and sometimes it took longer, but overall it seemed to work. The same principle could be applied to the pay rate for jobs. The IRS already has an index for all job types for example. It would not be hard to compile the average and upper rates paid for most job categories in the US and establish guidelines for how much people in these jobs should be paid. I have seen people locked in their job for years that are underpaid. When all service providers are required to disclose their rates workers can view a nationwide chart to see if they are being adequately paid.

The system will advise workers how much others in their position are being paid locally, regionally, and nationally. It will also indicate how much the job pays in a struggling company, a moderately growing company, and highly successful companies. If the worker is not being paid with those ranges they can complain to the Department of Labor.

A Traditional Work Week

When I was young most all companies paid overtime for anything over 40 hours per week. Later, some companies paid a premium for night work and for work done on weekends and certainly for work done on holidays. As the workforce moved more from factories to the office buildings in America that changed. Many workers were put on salary and no mention was made about overtime. I have seen workers not only work over 40 hours without overtime pay but do so without any notice. That would not happen in a 1950's factory job. The work schedules did not change much but if they did it generally required it to be put on the schedule the week before. If someone was absent or an emergency came up then management would *ask* a worker if they would work over. They often would do this as they too understood the situation and they would get paid extra to do it. It all worked as each side has some power. Today the workers have zero power, at least in states like Georgia.

Uniform Worker Benefits and Protections

Rather than using the union system which is hit and miss as they are hard to establish and it varies from state to state, why not have a uniform set of rules that would protect workers nationwide? Here is a list of stipulations that combine the best from each state, past and present:

First, workers are to have overtime pay for all work done over forty hours and all work done on holidays, nights, and weekends.

There shall be a seniority system in advancements. An employee cannot be fired after ninety days without cause.

All workers must be paid at least as much as the national pay scale for their type of work.

There must be equal pay for equal work (gender equality).

The minimum hourly wage shall not fall lower than three times the poverty level. Wage minimums are automatically adjusted annually, indexed to the cost of living.

There shall be four weeks of vacation per year.

Mothers shall have four weeks paid maternity leave for two occurrences. Fathers shall have two weeks paid leave for two occurrences.

Customer Database and Feedback

Yelp and other site are doing a pretty good job of ranking the quality of general work done, but this information must become more widely available and uniformly available so the question is do we wait to see it the marketplace expands so everyone can get this information or do we ask the government to require business people to list their goods and services along with the price and require them to provide a place online for customers to rank their satisfaction after the sale or service?

A Slightly Less Commercial Society

Along with a more equitable work arrangements we could benefit from a less commercial society. The current business model is fraught with pressures and tensions to meet sale goals, increase profits, lower costs and on and on. Some of this is what gives a business an edge but often business goes overboard and places unrealistic goals and responsibilities on employees.

Customer Service

In the continual effort for corporations to produce more profits they have reduced customer service from what it was when I was young. No longer do companies feel the need to have real-life people in local offices to address questions or problems for customers. Later it went to phone customer service and then from phone customer service to overseas phone technicians who live in developing countries where the wage costs are lower. There are many goods and services sold today where there is no human being involved at all. You order it online. If you have a problem you send an email and a return is set up. You simply mail it back.

I first wrote about this in the 1990's when the local gas company closed its offices and offered only phone support. They may have had trucks and utility people in the areas for repairs but there was no office for paying bills or talking to someone eyeball to eyeball if there was a problem. I think much of the world has grown accustomed to this and maybe the public at large has made an adjustment to this type of world. I still think there is value in human contact and I would say in the future all goods and services sold without support options should fall into the category of having to offer a full refund if the customer is dissatisfied. That is the trend among the largest on lines companies now. In the long run it costs them less money. This could work out if we can keep pushing the scale toward the customer getting a full refund when they are dissatisfied with the goods and services they have purchased.

Customer Satisfaction or a Full Refund

In the future all goods and services should come with a warranty of satisfaction or your money back. This would apply to both goods and services. Statistics would be available for every good, service, and supplier with a satisfaction rating by actual number of transactions like they do for items on E-Bay. With most people using credit and debit cards it will be easy to freeze or cancel sales when customers are dissatisfied.

Inundated with Commercialism

Everywhere we look we are inundated with advertising. Advertisers have long known that repetition is the way to impress a product or product information into the minds of potential buyers. In cable movies they run the same commercial over and over to imprint their message into the minds of those viewing. We must pull away from this. Advertising is everywhere including on the shirts of athletes, on billboards as we drive, on TV and radio, in our magazine publications and everywhere in between. Not only is most of our mail unsolicited advertising, but we are five years into routinely receiving scam calls on our phone with no legislation in sight to stop it.

If you have ever tried to reserve a website name you have discovered almost every name has been taken. That is because unscrupulous people have bought up the names at the basic rate and will not release them unless the purchaser pays some outrageous price. They often ask five or ten thousand dollars. We simply need a less greedy society. It has become about making companies successful regardless of what they do to society.

Last, in the past medical and legal professions were not allowed to advertise. I think it was restricted by the medical and legal professional societies. I wonder why they thought to do that and are consumers better off that today both professions fill the airways promoting themselves? I know there were laws preventing the advertising of alcoholic beverages and later cigarettes. At holiday time you can see a few ads for alcoholic beverages but never for cigarettes. Keeping items that are bad for our health works for me just as I would support preventing ads from exploiting consumers through repetition or through misinformation about their products.

Chapter 8- Healthcare

The cost for single health insurance premiums can run $8,900.00 annually while insurance for a family of four is reported as high as $24,400.00 per year. Healthcare spending accounts for at least a quarter of the entire federal budget and almost 20 percent of the private spending in this country. We are spending up to twice as much as any other developed nation, yet America is not the leader in quality healthcare nor is the public near the top in overall healthiness. Our medical care system costs twice that of Canada and one and a half times that of England, yet we have inferior care and lower health levels than those in other countries. Fewer Americans live above the age of 75 and our mortality rates for children are not better than some third world countries.

We all know there are problems but we do not have a consensus on what to do about it. Healthcare is not in the supply and demand of the free market. When you are on a steel table in the emergency room you are in no position to question pricing. A market will charge what the buyer can afford to pay and insurance has enabled people to pay more so the prices have gone up continually each year. It has escalated to an unreasonable point.

In the current system there are insurance deductibles along with co-pays that are so high you still owe your life's savings once you leave the hospital after a serious stay. There has to be a better way.

As a society we may have come to the point where Healthcare has outstripped the ability of the free market to allow healthcare insurance to be workable. In apples-to-apple comparisons, operations can often be performed overseas for about half the cost of an operation in America.

It has become so widely known that companies have sprang up to assist people in going overseas to have operations that would be unaffordable here at home. Insurance companies are working in concert with large employers by arranging what has become known as 'medical tourism' where patients are flown overseas and stay in nice hotels to have access to overseas medical care.

A friend moved to Ecuador to get affordable health insurance years ago and reports that a private healthcare policy for him and his wife combined is $67 per month. He says a colonoscopy and endoscopy costs were less than 10% of what they would cost in the U.S. and the procedures and care received were much better than the last two times he had them done in the U.S. Most of the developed countries have some form of universal healthcare and despite what critics say about it here at home people in those countries seem to like it.

Here in America, change has proven to be divisive. For people who like the free-market system understand the market will charge the maximum amount the market will bear. Insurance enables the medical industry to increase prices. However, over time the premiums have reached the level of being one of the top expenses in most families. Putting more money in the medical system has had some benefits in research and improved service but all along the way people in each medical sector receive high incomes, not just the doctors. It is the nature of the free market beast. Even in small towns the CEO of a public hospital makes well over a million and a half dollars salary per year. This is the case in my hometown, and the assistant makes $750.000.00 per year. This tells volumes about the high costs of healthcare.

Although healthcare insurance coverage has clearly become more universal through The Affordable Care Act, there seems to be little happening in the field of healthcare costs.

As reported in a national weekly magazine a cancer patient was required to produce $8,700.00 in cash before they would start his life-saving treatment. The kicker is that the patient already had insurance. The total bill was $83,000.00 but they would not begin the treatments until the deductible was produced. It turns out that the cost of the actual medication that was so expensive cost $300.00 wholesale.

When America has an industry with this outlook it needs to be gutted and rebuilt from scratch. The first consideration is to go back to non-profit healthcare. Second, we need to look at universal healthcare. Currently, the free enterprise myth of excellence remains a roadblock as the rest of the world continues happily with better and less expensive healthcare.

Universal Healthcare is More Efficient and Less Costly

The World Health Organization ranked the American healthcare system 37th in the world and the Commonwealth Fund ranked America's healthcare system last. Most other countries in the world offer universal approaches to healthcare and the result is lower costs, greater efficiency, and more equity. Primarily, the American healthcare system is more expensive because of the enormous costs of administering a private competitive system with over a thousand different policies with people at every level. It is inherently more expensive to figure out how to administer the individual policies, check the coverage, and then submit bills to the insurance companies for payments.

Until 2022 the government was not allowed to negotiate the price of prescriptions and in many cases is not allowed to use its buying power to force down prices. Other countries do not allow public advertising to consumers as was the practice in America until recently. Here are some of the highlights of countries that have universal coverage:

Australia has universal coverage but it encourages a private system for upper income earners by enforcing an additional

1% tax on them if they use the public system. It offers cradle-to-grave healthcare for everyone and covers most or all the costs for physician consultations, as well as specialists' fees and X-rays and pathology tests. Treatment in public hospitals is free.

Sweden spends approximately nine percent of its GDP on healthcare every year as compared to 16 percent in America. The Swedish healthcare system is publicly funded and largely decentralized. The government has taken great measures to allow every resident access to heavily subsidized healthcare services. Sweden utilizes healthcare centers to receive medical care that employ different medical specialists and thus offer different kinds of health services to their patients. The patients, on the other hand, are free to choose their doctor or healthcare facility as they please.

The French universal healthcare system is largely financed by a government national healthcare insurance program. Around 77 percent of the healthcare costs are covered by the state. France spends less than half of what America spends on healthcare per GDP. Most of their medical bills are taken care of by the government and the remaining expenses are paid for by the individual's supplemental private insurance. Every citizen is entitled to public coverage and now undocumented immigrants are covered as well. It is paid for from payroll and income taxes.

In the United Kingdom healthcare covers preventative services and mental healthcare. Most prescriptions there are exempt from charges. The United Kingdom ranked first on indicators of efficiency in the Commonwealth study.

Germany has the oldest universal healthcare system in the world with highly popular, quick, and high-quality service. German healthcare costs about half as much as in the American system with about the same level of care. Nine out of ten people use the public system with about ten percent using a private system.

Holland has compulsory healthcare but it is provided by private insurers competing for business. Overall it offers a high level of quality and fast service.

Canada's national healthcare system consists of a centralized body that sets standards that the 13 Canadian provinces must follow to receive funding. Hospitals are mainly private nonprofit organizations with their own governance structures.

Japan has universal healthcare with mandatory participation funded by payroll taxes paid by both employer and employee, or income-based premiums by the self-employed. Long-term care insurance is also required for those over forty.

In Taiwan, nearly every one of the country's 23 million residents are covered. Taiwan spends 6.5 percent of its gross domestic product on healthcare and more than 80 percent of the population is happy with the system. One hundred percent of the population is covered.

The Israeli healthcare system requires that citizens have at least basic insurance coverage at one of the country's four HMOs, with 80 percent of the population belonging to the two largest. The government has control over prices and puts strict regulations in place.

Spain's single-payer healthcare system is a highly ranked system that offers universal coverage and no out-of-pocket expenses other than prescription drugs. Some procedures do have a waiting list.

In America, insurance companies try to curb increased costs but they can only make providers charge about what everyone else is charging in the area and over time the prices inch upward. Insurance companies also had to increase deductibles and copays and they do it by raising out of pocket expenses to the highest rate a patient could afford to pay if they were hospitalized. In that view we are back to where we would be if insurance had never existed as no industry can sustain operations if they charge more than people can pay. So now we are stuck in a system where the money we pay into insurance is just gone and we, the insured patients, still must pay all the money we can afford toward co-pays and deductibles.

Hillary Clinton tried to do something about healthcare when she was the first lady and was slandered so badly by the medical industry it is a wonder she ever recovered. Later, with the problem still looming, candidate Barack Obama ran for office saying he would implement a universal, single payer insurance program. However, it seemed to never come up after the election. Once the program was finally developed after two years of wrangling and continual political turmoil the public was less than satisfied with the results of the Healthcare act.

Despite the concerns of critics about any publicly funded service, the conclusion of those who study such things is that publicly funded healthcare systems deliver better healthcare and deliver it at a lower cost. In universal healthcare the government can negotiate the prices for medical services. This was done in Japan and prices were lowered by thirty percent. Replacing one thousand private insurance provider's varying policies with a single payer policy system would save the American consumers about 200 to 400 million dollars per year and would include covering everyone with better coverage. With this kind of money at stake and possibly the entire healthcare insurance industry worried, it is easy to see why the healthcare industry overpower congressmen on both sides of the aisle.

Many people (and some medical doctors) say that medical malpractice costs are a factor in driving up the costs of healthcare. However studies show that it accounts for less than ten percent of the overall costs. If people want to address the medical malpractice costs, do it in a way that does not penalize the victims who rightfully bring lawsuits. Lower the legal costs that are added to legal claims that are so high. Medical suits tend to have high awards because of the nature of the damage (a person's life or their health) and because the doctors make high incomes. Lawyers take this opportunity to work on a contingency fee basis by offering to go to court without charging the victim any money up front. If they win the case the lawyer charges a third to a half of all the money in the award. This is factored in, so basically the amount of the award sought by victims is doubled. Lawyers have ruined their own industry with their voracity. The way to resolve this is by placing limits on how much lawyers can charge.

While some of us fall into the misfortune of an illness or a disease, a report shows that in the daily routine of office visits there is just too much money pushing around too few illnesses. Overall, we are a healthy society and could be even healthier if we ate more nutritiously and exercised more. If you go to the doctor's office twice a year you're going to get a prescription and eventually they will find something wrong with you. The lab reports eventually show something alarming, then there comes another prescription only to find out a few years later it was not that critical. No matter what your health status is, if you can pay, they want to see you back in six months. Those in their critical years (the young and the elderly) can benefit from such checkups but those in the middle need only go every two years and maybe even once every four years. Many people just can't take 'yes' for an answer. If you're healthy, move on. It is not just an opinion; it is also the conclusion from a medical study published in the American Medical Journal.

Paying for Healthcare

It should be stipulated that healthcare for Americans should not cost more than the same care available in other developed nations. If we look at the costs in other countries and look at the discounts one can leverage through negotiations we can save roughly half the cost of our current healthcare. Many people have reservations about universal healthcare because it is a socialist type of program. Universal healthcare advocates like it because it costs less and generally results in better healthcare. Universal healthcare is the choice, in one form or another, of virtually every other developed nation in the world. If you have in mind another system or method that will save 25 percent to 50 percent of our current system, as is said of universal healthcare, people will listen to your proposals. No one has yet to have any other plan.

There was a moment in the 2020 presidential election when Joe Biden claimed Sanders' universal insurance plan would take the choice out of the hands of individual Americans who may like their current insurance plan and company. I can't imagine anyone liking their private insurance carrier but putting that aside Sanders didn't effectively drive home the obvious that private insurance has deductibles that are often unaffordable and there are limitations on what they cover and so on. Biden won the election and universal Healthcare is not on the table as of this writing. Further, corporations are buying up all the hospitals (public and private) so it is unclear what is on the horizon. Given where the country is now I'd address the need for choice in this way. Let everyone keep their current insurance if they want it. However, allow the government to offer a new insurance program sponsored by the federal government and operated by a separate agency like how the post office is set up. Make the premiums about half what people are paying now and free for those who are now on federal or state welfare programs and medical services. Use the funding from the money that is currently given to the individual states to pay for healthcare of the poor since they are automatically entered into this program. As citizens see the value of the program (as it is half the price) the program will grow and revenue will increase. Before long, most people will be on board and the program will pay for itself.

Medications

In general, America pays twice as much as any other country for the same medications. It would be a start if the government would regulate prescription costs to restrict companies from charging US customers more than they charge overseas customers for the same medicines.

Further, why do we allow pharmacies to charge one customer more than another for the same drug? When we buy milk it is not one price for some while others pay less because some organization negotiated a better price for its members. That is in essence how insurance works by negotiating with providers. It is less expensive to serve the cash paying customer as no billing is required to receive payment. It would work out better to charge everyone the same for the same pill and have the price established by an independent agency of the government like they do in Japan. Having the government negotiate for medical service has worked out well here in the U.S. for Medicare services. That is why some people simply advocate for "Medicare for all."

Mental Health America

We also have a societal interest in the mental health of individuals in society. Not only from the perspective of individual happiness and contentment as a nicety, but to minimize the number of people who might have inner demons that may cause them to break the rules of society with violence and crime. We need to have therapy and counseling available for everyone, as well as have routine small screening sessions when we go for a physical check-up.

We live in a society where, if lucky and healthy, life is comfortable. However, people still have social problems, problems finding contentment, happiness, and unable to blend into society. Some of us are still suffering from things that may have happened in childhood. If you argue with your spouse, your children, your boss, and workmates continually or if you are a disconnected loner it is not good for our society as a whole or for those involved around you. Having a mental health professional to talk to on the phone, on the Internet, and where needed, in person can help society flow easier and progress more. It does not hurt to have someone to call once a month just to stay in touch. If we all had a mental checkup like we do for physicals it would be great screening and it would also help remove any leftover stigma from the past about opening up on personal issues.

In 1963, President Kennedy signed the Community Mental Health Act aimed to build 1,500 mental health centers around the country to improve mental Healthcare. It brought positive changes but was never fully funded. Some of our citizens have more serious mental health needs than others. If we would devote more of our resources to address these problems we might save ourselves some of the grief of these national tragedies that we see unfold in the senseless shootings that have been all too prevalent from school shootings, shootings in public places, and so many local tragedies that do not make the national newspapers or the evening news.

Many of these mental and social problems we carry all throughout life start in childhood and often develop in school. In the education section of the book is the concept of a "group of five." If school children were grouped together in groups of five they would have a base group of relationships with other children. The school would be matching children with others that are reasonably compatible. The teacher could require these groups to be polite and civil with each other and they could have several basic responsibilities like keeping up with homework assignments and being sure they all returned from recess and lunches on time, etc. If a child was not blending in it would very likely show up early where something could be done about it.

Chapter 9- Banking

As corporations are legally 'people' they must be good citizens like the rest of us. Both business and consumers must be healthy for the relationship to be beneficial and indeed possible. Companies should have social consciousness and none more so than those who are dominant in the marketplace. Banks fall into this category of institutions that so very much dominate their consumers.

Credit Cards

There is a long trail of centralized banks taking all the money out of the communities in this country. Decades ago banks began offering credit cards from out-of-state banks making inroads on local banks. From the first, credit cards were easy to get. Applications for credit cards came in the mail several times a week for most Americans until everyone had one or more. Today the average person has eight credit cards. Of the 600 million credit cards in circulation, over 100 million of our citizens only make the minimum payment with an average balance around eight thousand dollars.

In the late 1970's and early 1980's capital was hard to come by for banks. They had to offer up to twenty-five percent interest to attract depositors. Most states had usury laws that capped interest rates on savings accounts to around fourteen percent. Citibank of New York determined it was not making money on credit cards and claimed it was a loss leader for their other banking services. To make money in this increasing market the bank offered to move their credit card operations to the isolated state of South Dakota if it removed the usury laws that were in place to protect the consumer from unscrupulous banking practices. However, it was not the financial conquest of sparsely populated South Dakota that the New York bank had in mind. The courts ruled that usury laws of a state did not control the rates of banks that were headquartered in other states that allowed higher interest charges. This had unwittingly cleared the way for central banks to take over state banking because they could offer their services nationwide. Citibank moved its credit card operations to South Dakota and several other banks located there before Delaware and other states modified their laws and removed the usury caps as they were seeing all the development in South Dakota.

Once the usury laws were removed the banks shifted to a revolving style card that did not require full payoff each month. The balance could be carried forward. Not only could the banks charge higher interest, but they charged the higher interest longer with the balances that were carried over. Credit cards went from being marginal items for banks to the top center of profits. The banking industry was about to change and change American life with it.

Anyone who gets mail knows that credit cards are available with low introductory rates. We are always pre-approved, but for some reason there is a form to fill out and a disclaimer that credit may not be extended. In other words it is a lie that we would not be able to get away with (or want to try) but banks do it on such a big scale we accept it for some reason. They offer a low rate and once you are using the card they up the rate to as much as three times the introductory rate. Later interest rates are as high as 24 to 29 percent.

Republican President George Bush Sr. tried to get a national cap on interest rates. A senate committee passed President Bush's measure with broad support, but the house looked at a slight drop in the stock market and used that for cover and did not take up the measure. It was dropped and has never been brought forward again. Occasionally a congressperson will try to get a national usury law passed but they find they are out maneuvered by powerful lobbies.

Most adults who deal with money know the pitfalls of having credit cards. Few embrace the companies that send the monthly bills, but few of us can do without their services. In fact, while cash is generally accepted, fewer and fewer places today will accept a personal check. Today I suppose some of the younger people in our society have never written a check. It used to be the standard way to convey money. Today, one must have either a credit card or debit card. The first thing all customers must come to terms with is the mammoth difference in the leverage the bank has on the individual customer. Credit card issuers start out with an agreement that many lawyers could not fully understand, but we all understand we are signing away our rights to have credit. The banks and card issuers have all the control. It is an unequal relationship and while valid, contracts are supposed to be an agreement between parties where both understand and agree to the terms. Among the 'terms' we agree the card issuers may change the terms at any time with fifteen days' notice, including the interest rates. That is amazing. They can also charge annual fees, too..

Cardholders do have minimum protections. Generally one can close the account and pay a card off under the old terms. Few card holders know this as it is buried in the small print. Plus, the banks understand their customers. They know that one hundred million people only pay the minimum balances each month and they need credit to get them through their monthly expenses of living so they can hardly go without a credit card. Plus they know few will even read the notices they send out with all the small print. It might be months before card holders notice a different rate is being applied and often they can charge an annual fee and it is not even noticed.

It is not hard to get an increase in the limit on credit card balances as the banks use revolving account methods that only require about two percent of the outstanding balance to be paid down each month. The rest of the payment is interest. They want card holders to carry high balances so they can charge high interest. They claim the higher interest is justified as the cards are unsecured. But a credit card company can go to court and attach anything you own of value to cover non-payments, so how is that unsecured? It is secured by everything you own. If they want to claim they are unsecured, it should be clear in the law that they cannot attach anything to recover unpaid balances. That would solve a lot of problems as banks would no longer extend credit so easily nor raise the limits so high.

Home Loan Lenders

In the old days, most banks were locally owned. They would loan money for home mortgages and carry the note 'in-house' where the loans were made. Each bank had a loan committee that would approve or not approve a loan. Being local and knowing they were carrying the note till the end they would be sure it was a good risk in that, one, the person getting the loan would likely repay and two, if they did not, the home would be worth the mount of the outstanding balance would be at least twenty percent less than the value of the home. Everything worked well enough under this system until the explosion of interstate banking. Now banks do business over state lines and can be nationwide. Many stockholders of local banks made a lot of money selling to those large banks as they took over the banking market. Those local banks still make home loans, but they are not kept 'in house' as before. They are bundled and sold to speculators on Wall Street. That removes many of the safeguards discussed above.

Mortgage Interest

For most of my life I have debated the unfairness of the compound loan system. I maintain that compound home loans are front loaded with interest and more of the principal is paid toward the later part of the loan. I think it is unfair from this perspective. If you're five years into a $360,000 thirty-year loan and for whatever reason must sell the home or even default on the loan, you have paid more than your fair share of interest and not enough principle to reflect five years of payments. You're one-sixth of the way through the loan and should owe $300,000. But the banks say you owe $321,000 after you have paid for five years. They do this every day and have done it for decades. I think the principle and the interest should be of equal amounts all the way across the amortization table and not front loaded. Mortgage loans that have amortized each monthly payment to have half interest and half principle will give the homeowner more incentive to keep the home by giving them more ownership each month. It will also help them get out from under loans when needed as the principal amount owed will be less. There are reasons working people do not get ahead and this, in my opinion, is one of them. Banks get to make the rules…so far.

Resuming Rate Caps

When two parties sit down to negotiate a loan or credit line, individuals are out manned by the organized interests of large banks and cannot negotiate anything. It is 'take it or leave it.' However, if the borrowers could get together in a room with all the banking industry they would outnumber them immensely and would have the leverage to get more reasonable terms. We as consumers need to organize to either elect officials who will do this on our behalf or be afforded a consumer union to negotiate the terms of credit as a group. Our elected leaders are supposed to do this for us, but if their elections are funded by special interests the public will come second. For some reason we have grown to accept this. We shouldn't.

The first thing consumers would want to establish are baseline rates for interest charges for all lines of consumer credit. The constant up and down of the market most often works against the consumer as their income is fixed. They cannot adjust their income weekly like the financial markets. During one of America's most prosperous periods, the home mortgage rate was four percent and less. Four percent should be the standard cap unless there is runaway inflation, insufficient deposits, or an inability of the Federal Reserve to loosen the money supply.

The other prime consideration is the fear of losing bank business to other states that offer higher interest rate caps. Even though it hurts their citizens, many states offer extremely high interest rate caps. The best solution is to elect people who will establish a national usury limit like George Bush tried to get passed.

The credit card rate could be established at a slightly higher rate with a five percent cap. It might seem low to speculators but they will continue to lend. If they slowed lending it would encourage savings as people cannot pull out their credit card each time they see something that catches their eye. Less consumer spending on consumable items will also prevent some inflation tendencies and slow the economy. It would reduce the personal debt in this country, which many point to as a sign of financial weakness.

The Housing Committee on Banking and Currency said in 1956 that "a four and a half percent interest rate is a fair rate for a virtually riskless investment." At the same time they recognized that discounts to some degrees are unavoidable and indeed are a necessary adjustment to changing supply and demand relationships. They pointed out the without caps interest rates would rise and that it could be controlled by one of two methods. Either the market could establish the rate by looking at the competitive position of each bank or the banks could look at the average collection of interest made on deposits and make loans slightly higher to make a profit. Of the two methods, the 'mark-up theory' seems to offer the most stability and the most assurances that the consumer's welfare will be served. Keeping treasury yields at a lower rate will ensure the system of enough capital to serve the demand for loans. Instead of panicking each time the market fluctuates, which leads to even more instability, let the market have certainty of consumer interest rates and treasury yields to help calm financial swings in the market.

The answer for banks having a high percentage of defaults on their home mortgages is to make better loans, to not lend more than a property is worth, and last to require banks to have the liability over the term of the loan. On revolving credit the answer is for the banks to extend lower limits on each credit card. At the height of my business days I had one credit card with a $55,000 limit and one with a $35,000 limit. Among my department store cards was a $6,000 card from a clothing store. None of those limits make any sense other than the card issuers know that there are fewer write-offs than people who will charge their cards and pay the high interest. The banks are willing to live with the defaults, but it hurts the entire economy when too many people are paying high interest over a long period for consumable items and items that often have short term benefits. The only intuitive way to curtail this harm is to increase the liability of the card issuer so they will not extend unwarranted risks. It is essential that lenders do not have the right to attach other property or garnish wages. It will truly make the credit cards unsecured short-term loans, just as the banks have been intimating all these years.

Inflation

The financial tool used to curb inflation is to raise interest rates. I have never liked it as it is a direct punitive tool that punishes the average rank and file citizen while adding to the profit of the banks and large institutions. In February of 2022 rate changes made the cost of a middle-class home increase over $300.00 per month. That loan will be with the buyer for the term of the loan no matter what the economy does over the next thirty years. That is a $300.00 monthly burden the buyer of similar homes did not have if they purchased the previous month or earlier. There must be a better way.

I know when I make a little money I take that opportunity to pay off some or all of my debts. The Federal Reserve holds about 35 percent of the national debt so I wonder why the Fed does not take the opportunity to pay down some of the national debt even if they must set the funds aside until the economy cools down. It is all complicated. At least there will be money available if any of these changes I have proposed temporary stalls the economy. If it is thought that they might have that effect, then this inflationary time in our economy is a good time to put some of them into place.

Financial Privacy

Things have changed so much in my lifetime and none more than the data collection of people's private financial information. Naturally, a lender wants to know everything possible about a loan applicant and that is true of credit card issuers also. But there seems to be no limit on how far they would intrude into our lives. America rose up to be the most powerful nation in the world without collecting such data and one wonders why we allow it now. Having the information displayed to virtually anyone in finance is too little personal privacy and the history goes back too far. We notice that many companies do not report good payments, just bad ones. It is more than difficult to correct an inaccurate report and the system is so harsh to those who fail to live up to the market standards, standards the market elite do not live up to themselves. Credit reporting should just go away, but certainly the market could continue to operate efficiently if credit reports were limited to the past three years of a person's credit.

Chapter 10- Making Justice Obtainable

The court system is overly complex and overly expensive. Justice should not be so unattainable for so many people. We could have a system where the court appoints attorneys for civil and criminal hearings. Lawyers could make a decent living by earning a $150.00 filing fee plus $150.00 per hour maximum with $1,000 maximum for legal preparation work.

Magistrate and lower court appearances could be billed out at $150.00 per hour with a cap to limit the bill from getting too high for what is basically an argument of some sort. Lawyers like to take contingency cases because they can get a part of the award in cases where the victim cannot pay their hourly rates. This just adds to the cost of the award. Contingency fees should be limited to five percent of the award plus hourly reimbursement if they win. In the end, this system will almost pay for itself and more people will be able to afford justice.

The law is not that complicated and what is complicated about going to court is not taught in law school. Anyone who can clear the bar exam should be able to practice law. As a compromise they might need to complete a self-study, internet study program, or work under a lawyer as an apprentice as was done in the past. They could become like journeymen before going out on their own if needed. This was the system in the old days.

Chapter 11- A New Tax Structure

A Flat Income Tax

Earlier we established that companies would pay a twenty percent flat rate income tax and that smaller, micro businesses, would pay taxes at the ten percent rate. These lower taxes reflect the profit sharing of companies from being in worker/owner partnerships. Continuing with the flat rate federal income tax codes here are the flat rate income tax rates for individuals and companies in all other forms of earnings whether they are active or passive in a graduated scale:

10 percent tax rate for incomes to 100K
15 percent tax rate for incomes to 500K
20 percent tax rate for incomes from 500K

And we should respect the rich for paying 20 percent of their earnings to make society function. Today it is speculated that certain companies like Amazon pay no taxes, but ordinary corporations currently pay about 20 percent in taxes on their profits. Also, marriage status or how one files will not be needed. There would be no categories for filing jointly or head of household. As noted all passive income, lottery, and gambling winnings would be taxed at the flat rate. 'Loopholes' and deductions are no longer needed for business as the rates have been lowered. The home mortgage deduction is no longer needed because interest rates have been lowered and stabilized by law. Hopefully, there will be little or no tax on primary homes if they are of ordinary size and value. Inheritance taxes would only apply on estates that are valued at more than ten million dollars. Do note that all these tax figures are the 'effective rate' which means that it is the actual percentage of tax due on profits as opposed to tax brackets. In our changing world if this these flat tax rates leave a shortfall in revenue, the next tax brackets would be 12, 20, and 30 percent.

Advertising Deduction

I would also remove advertising as a tax deduction for all areas other than pure advertising in media. I would disallow it in sports or other promotions where the advertising or sponsorship might further a personal interest of the company or its owners.

Minimum Tax

The corporate alternative minimum tax was introduced in 1986 and it was repealed in 2017. It was reinstated I 2022 and we will have to see how it is implemented and how large corporations deal with it. No matter how many deductions a high earner or a large corporation may have at no time shall their tax burden be less than five percent of sales or assets.

So all filers will pay from five percent to a maximum of 35 percent of all their federal, state, and local taxes.

Home Mortgage Deduction

The mortgage interest deduction was instituted to encourage home ownership. However the way it is applied allows the banks to charge more interest, so there is little gain for the consumer because people are charged what they can afford to pay in our society. When the government gives the homeowner a deduction on the interest, it allows lenders to charge more because homeowners can pay more. So, in the end, deductions do not save the citizens money.

There is No Additional Tax Burden on the Middle or Working Class People in this Book.

In all this tax structure and in all the various plans and proposals in this book none call for an increase on the middle or working class in America. The Healthcare 'tax' is a replacement to the much higher Healthcare premium. The only possible caveat is the proposal for a national tariff of one percent on all goods and services imported into the United States. For comparison, the Trump administration imposed a 16.8 percent tariff on similar goods in 2020. From time to time he imposed a 25 percent tariff on certain goods. President Biden has also placed tariffs on imports including a 25 percent tariff on steel and a whopping 100 percent tariff on electric vehicles from China. Currently there is an average two percent tariff on half the incoming goods and the remainder are duty free. A one percent tariff would be manageable and the programs discussed in this book institute no great burden on the middle and working classes of this country.

For whatever reason there are many defenders of the rich who do not want them taxed at higher rates even if the taxes are minimal in the context of their overall wealth or overall tax burden. Perhaps they think one day they are going to be among them but the odds are that you are not rich today in America you are not going to become rich. America has become stale. The odds of economic improvement are greater in Bolivia than they are in the United States and there are more millionaires being made in China today than in the United States.

So we seek to reorganize governmental activities and public aims toward building a robust middle class. America has drifted away from this focus and we should return to focusing on the middle class and the American dream. Those that achieve extraordinary incomes and wealth will still be prevalent in the United States and we are happy to have them as they contribute toward America but they will pay a slightly elevated tax rate for the privilege and joys of being better off than the average American. The rich are the ones that can best shoulder the burden of these changes and the sums asked for are in proportion to their wealth and should not materially change their lifestyle or status. There are a few super rich among us who have avoided paying their fair share and they will see a change but most all taxes are on profits and income to begin with and while paying taxes may affect the numbers on their wealth tabulations they will remain super rich. Some of that tax shall go toward helping to grow the middle class and to diminish the number of poor till the number of poor falls below five percent.

A One Quarter of One Percent Tax on the Highest One Percent of Earners

One way of raising funds for these programs and other programs to end poverty, hunger, and to end human violence in the USA and around the world is a simple tax of one-quarter of one percent on the income and assets of those in the very highest percentile of income and wealth. That is, for those making 360,000 dollars they would incur a $900.00 tax. When looking at the very rich, income doesn't always tell the story. For example, Jeff Bezos who is on track to be the first Trillionaire has claimed an annual salary of under $100,000.00 for decades. For this category of people we must look at assets and income. With a net worth of almost 200 billion dollars, Jeff Bezos will be asked to pay five hundred million in tax for American and world improvement. That is a lot of money that 'we' are taking from the entrepreneur but it is about the same amount he paid for his last yacht and again it is 'only' one quarter of one percent of his wealth. The "Wealth Tax" would stay in place for as long as more than five percent of the population found themselves struggling to have the basics for living on our planet.

With these funds there will be enough money to end hunger worldwide and begin to address the slum conditions in every part of the world. Programs to provide housing and other basic services like health care will be available to each citizen of the world...and more. All the while, we will be teaching the value of being self-reliant and self-supporting so struggling individuals will not be a continual burden to society.

Possible One Percent Tariff

There is, too, a one percent tariff on U.S. imports that would raise an additional 30 billion dollars if it is needed. That cost will be spread to all of us rich and poor alike. These figures do not include the international support that an international movement should garner from other developed countries. In the scheme of things it would be a large undertaking that would probably benefit from being in a new department of government for implementation.

Even in taxing the billionaires ''we' should limit taxation to that highest level of the rich have paid before. In the 1980's it is reported the rich paid an effective rate of around 40 percent. That is a lot by today's standards. Back then corporations and the wealthy paid the bulk of the federal income tax. Today that is no longer the case thanks mostly to Ronald Reagan. He wanted the rich to pay less and today they are said to have an effective rate of around 27 percent, but I would not bet on that. Many large corporations pay in the low teens and we all see from year to year that several large corporations and notable rich pay nearly nothing or no taxes at all.

Tax Collection

Today many are calling for a new tax code and calling for various methods of collecting taxes that they find more equitable. To begin with, let the government put the tax software on the internet so that people can use an updated method to figure out how much they owe under the current system of complicated laws. It is only asking to recognize that we now live in the computer age not the paper age. They provide paper forms but every taxpayer must either hire someone to do their taxes or buy tax software that is about $30.00 for individuals or at least $69.00 for small businesses. I am sorry for the negative impact on the tax software companies who make several billion dollars per year providing this service, but the computerized forms should appear on the internet from the IRS for free, including being able to compute deductions for both individuals and companies. They want the money; they should at least provide the software. This is for the current system. Under a flat tax system the software would be quite simple as there are no deductions.

The IRS did propose a new approach to taxation once. They said it would be easier and more efficient to send everyone a bill each year for the amount they thought was due rather than have the taxpayer fill out long forms and do calculations trying to figure out how much the IRS was expecting. They certainly collect enough information to verify we are reporting correctly so why not have them send us a bill just like the utility companies? There was heavy lobbying by the companies that sell tax software and conservatives that didn't trust the IRS to send out a fair bill. The IRS had stipulated that they would send out the bill and if there was any concern that it was too high the taxpayer could still itemize and send in the tax forms as in the past. In a new flat tax system with no need for deductions, a simple bill that could come monthly, quarterly, or yearly, is all that would be needed.

Homestead Exemptions

We want the economy to grow and government efficiency to increase until the government does not need to levy high property taxes on ordinary individual homes. Currently you cannot truly own property in most states because property taxes are so high it represents a constant need to save money each month for taxes. Although some states do not have property taxes at all and some have capped the level of taxation on homes. A cap limiting property taxes to a maximum of $500.00 for every $100,000.00 of property value would at least lessen the burden of taxation on home ownership.

In Georgia, there used to be a homestead exemption for the school tax portion for homeowners once they reached sixty-five years old. Recently, however, the Republican controlled state house increased that to a higher age for the exemptions. It would be nice if senior citizens could own an ordinary home and not have to pay property taxes in their later years. And too, it would be nice to have protection on primary residences where the spouse or partner died.

Social Security Tax

One would need to add the social security tax of five percent for both businesses and employees. The tax would be collected no matter the income level so without that limitation the system would be secure for years to come.

Wall Street Tax for School Loans

A Wall Street tax has been proposed by others and promoted in the Bernie Sanders campaign in 2020. Essentially, the under taxed Wall Street stocks would be taxed at one percent each time they were bought or sold. The money would go to defray current college tuition costs and to retire outstanding college debt. As of this writing, the outstanding debt is about 1.5 trillion dollars. In looking at other viewpoints, many people would accept the means tested version which would pay out depending on the income of the students or their family. The proceeds could be divided by allocating 40 percent toward current college tuition, means tested, and 40 percent toward old college debt for those who have lower incomes. The remaining 20 percent could go to lower income workers who struggled to pay back their loans but have them paid off. Versions of this are often discussed and circulated but the bottom line is the economy probably cannot survive if millions of students are paying the loans with their interests tacked onto them. Eventually this will become apparent.

Recently, the government has offered to write off school loans if students could show they were misled while in school with the promise of a job, etc. It's a start, but as of this writing those schools are mostly online schools that are highly marketed on TV and are still in business.

In 2024, which happens to be an election year, the Biden Administration put forth several plans to reduce or eliminate some student loan debt for some students.

Several people oppose any government assistance in this area. One argument is that their kids are not going to school so why should they pay? My answer is, first, your kids should go to school. Secondly, you probably don't have an airplane but the government builds private airports everywhere in America as well as hiking trail that you may or may not use and so on. That is how government works. You may not take advantage of all the services governments offer but you might be using a service that, say, students do not use. However, the most fundamental reason is this: school costs have gone up more than most all other sectors of the economy and certainly more than income. It varies by school, but costs have risen 7 times to ten times and more than when I attended school. In the '70's the cost for public college was under 5K and now they are 35K per year. I have seen no study that indicates less than a tripling of college costs. Some of this is because state governments are covering less of the bill as their conservative voter base doesn't value education as much as previous generations. At any rate, the most palatable way to pay off the school debt is to remove the cost from income tax collection and use Wall Street trading as the vehicle to raise funds. That way it is not coming from the working-class incomes.

Lottery Ticket Revenue for College Debt

There seems to be resistance to any effort to pay off student debt from some quarters. If there's a continued deadlock in agreeing on how to pay off the trillion dollars plus student loan debt then perhaps we could simply have another lottery offering where only people wanting to buy that particular lottery ticket would be contributing to paying down the debt. One idea is to make that lottery ticket pay out differently by having a winner each week as I talked about in the 'Lottery" section. It might catch on.

Part 3 - The Election System

Chapter 12 – Problems in the Election Process

Each election cycle brings with it a discussion on election reform to make political office holders more responsive to the electorate instead of the special interests who give them the money to run their campaigns. The thought is that the candidate who can run the most advertising can get their name out to the voting public and win the election. Perhaps more realistically they can run the most negative commercials and slander their opponent to the point no one wants to vote for them. With both candidates doing the same thing we end up with officials we already think of as scoundrels before they go into office and muck everything up. However, each time a reform has gained enough support to get passed into law the courts have ruled them an infringement of free speech. So we must look for ways to chip away at those who have made rank and file citizens unimportant in the political process. It seems there are problems at every stage of our political and civil system. Let's do something about all this. Now is the time.

Registration Fees are too Steep

The first thing a candidate for office must do is to file for candidacy and pay an entrance fee. The fee is small for most local and state offices but it is sizable in, say, Georgia to run for any federal office where the registration fee is about $5,000.00 to run for congress. That is a roadblock for many who might make good representatives but who are too prudent to risk that sum of money from family funds and if one must raise the money it often comes from special interests consisting of either business or single-issue interests. A more reasonable fee would be a thousand dollars maximum for the federal office.

Independent Candidates Must Collect Signatures

The fees are due from candidates in most states no matter if they are aligned into a political party or wish to run as an independent. However If you want to run as an Independent, you also have to collect signatures in most states where members of an established political party do not. While all states are a bit different, in Georgia, an independent candidate would have to collect about 10,000 signatures to qualify as a candidate in addition to paying the registration fee.

In the 1990's I worked for Ross Perot and we made it all look easy but behind the scenes it was a little more difficult and we had a billionaire who was well known and well liked. Of course, money for entrance fees was not a problem for Ross Perot. This year, 2024, Robert Kennedy Junior is making an independent run for the presidency and has found some difficulty getting on each state's ballot. He has put aside 15 million dollars to go to court in several states to force his way on the ballot in about a dozen states and to arrange for supporters to collect the needed signatures. He feels those states would be enough to put him over the top if he could win. The takeaway from his experience is that he had to spend, on average, a million dollars per state to get on the ballot. That is not democracy in any sense.

Political Parties

There are fewer things that could improve the political process more than doing away with the governmental sanctioning of political parties. For people or indeed elected officials to coalesce around issues is a fine thing. However, for the government to recognize them as an organization or political body is totally wrong. Most of us are so used to political parties that they take them for granted as being as legitimate as the three branches of government. Of course, if you really like one or the other political parties you may not object to their governmental affiliation. I do realize it is all most of us have ever experienced. It is easier to get into politics by running under a political banner. However the pitfalls are obvious. The good aspect is the candidate has some built in votes, the bad part is that it comes at the sacrifice of their independence. Once under the party banner, it is like being in the army, rarely do orders come from the bottom, there is a hierarchy of established leadership and their agenda is the one that is most often followed.

The constitution allows each state to formulate how they will send representatives to federal offices. It is curious that in every state they have decided to recognize successful political parties from the previous election and all others must collect signatures to get on the ballot. What makes it worse is that the federal government gives them money to hold their national political convention which surely must be illegitimate. The states support the primaries by having their election officers oversee the elections and pay to have election places and election machines to help the parties select their candidates. Currently, the government will match some contributions but the candidates must be members of a political party.

Clearly if candidates were not listed by political party (or listed as being the incumbent) each candidate would have a better chance of being elected and the advantage of being in a political party would be diminished. If political parties were no longer recognized on the ballots then gerrymandering would be less of a problem. That would cause some voters to study up before voting rather than just voting by party affiliation.

Ranked Voting

There are other ways to make the elections better. For example, the idea of 'ranked voting' where voters select two or more candidates for each office is seen as having many benefits but change is very hard to make in these areas. I read one paper that suggested allowing people to simply vote for every candidate they liked.

In our rural town in Georgia we have non-partisan elections for some of our local offices. If we need five commissioners and voters can vote for five candidates from a list that sometimes has seven to ten candidates. The top five vote-getters win. One does not have to say which party they affiliate with if any. I have noticed over the years that few of them tout any party affiliation. I like that aspect of it.

Ballot Verification System

The last decade brought several things into American life that was unexpected. I didn't foresee the day that a major American presidential candidate would claim an American election to have been illegitimate. If people are telling pollsters the truth, many people today now distrust election results and they have many concerns about aspects of voting. I was as shocked then as I am today that people I have known for decades would come into my office and question the election system and some would talk of a conspiracy and more. I suspect there are a number of people that would never except any voting system or vote unless their candidate won. However, if the problem is a question of a valid voting method a simple solution is available. Simply number the ballots.

Whether a district is using paper or electronic ballots this system will assure all voters that their ballot was recorded accurately and that it counted toward the results. Further it would show that only the people who went through the voter lines, mailed in a ballot, or voted online (where that is allowed) and that their vote, or any other, was only counted once.

Here is how it works. When a voter gets in line to vote they are handed a ballot (in paper voting) or they enter a computer booth. At the top of the ballot is a number. The first two digits indicate the state. The second two digits indicate the county. The next three digits indicate the precinct they are voting in and the last four digits the single voter as the ballots are numbered in order. When a person votes the ballot has that unique number. The vote is recorded under that number without any personal information about the voter. The voters need only keep up with that number. As the numbers are tabulated the results are listed on an official government website. At any time a voter can use that number to look up their vote as can every other voter. The number of votes cast cannot exceed the number of ballots given out. The proof the system works is that each number will correspond to the voters' preferences that received the number.

What many may not realize is that there are poll watchers at every voting precinct in America. They are there on behalf of the candidate or on behalf of a political party. The candidates (or political party) select these people. They can easily monitor the number of people voting in a precinct.

This numbering system could easily extend to computer voting as ballots would be numbered as the ballot is cast. You can access it from your registered name that is password protected. It is the same system you have that protects all your money at banks. You trust it for that so why not trust it for voting? Mail in ballots could simply be numbered as they are given out. You would remove the sticker that has the unique number. This solves the voting issues, but there are more things to tackle to have the political system we deserve.

The Fairness Doctrine

The Fairness Doctrine was a policy by the FCC that requires equal time in discussions of matters in public policies, proposed laws etc. It was first instituted in 1949 and was removed under Ronald Reagan in 1987. Several attempts were made, initially, with some bipartisan support, to put it back into law through congressional action throughout the years. George W. Bush said he would veto the measure if it were brought before him in the 1990's killing an attempt to put it into law and it was formally removed again with Republican support in 2011.

When it was removed in 1987 it gave rise to political talk radio and the 24-hour news channels. These outlets could give their slant to the issues of the day without concern for having someone following them offering corrections. This has given rise to a large element in the United States getting their 'news' from single or similar sources believing the propaganda put out by these talk radio and cable news channels. Few things have had a more detrimental effect on America in the last several decades than the dissemination of one-sided 'news' because of the removal of the Fairness Doctrine. These 24-hour news channels and talk radio programs are not informing the public, they are recruiting the public to a set of issues in a partisan and alarmist fashion. That cannot be understated. We now have half the country getting information which is no more than basic propaganda. I took an evening to watch one station and I was shocked how partisan the evening programs were, noting they were filled with half-truths, omissions, and every action they spoke of made it seem like the country was falling apart.

I would urge a reinstatement of the Fairness Doctrine but it would be a long haul now as these outlets have millions of dollars in revenues at stake and would wage a legal battle claiming free speech. Under the Fairness Doctrine they are allowed free speech but when using the public airwaves they are required to give equal time to opposing views. The Supreme Court has upheld this in the past. It would be interesting to see what the most conservative court in modern times would do with a case before it. The second method of reestablishing fairness is to have congress pass a law requiring it. That would give it more teeth in a legal battle.

Gerrymandering

Another critical problem blocking democracy is the gerrymandering of political districts. There are certain things that people understand are wrong, but they are so difficult to do anything about that people throw their hands up and look at other issues. Currently the Republicans are the ones who benefit from Gerrymandering. However, I suspect it would happen under Democrats too if they had control of the state houses who are currently in charge of drawing the districts. Today, more than any time before, technical data makes it possible to draw the district lines in such a way that the outcome of an election is almost a certainty. The geography is divided up right down to each street and each house. In at least six congressional districts across America the majority of the voters voted for Democratic candidates but because of the way the lines were drawn Republicans won the offices. Elected officials who are also members of political parties should be the last ones to have any part of drawing new districts.

Sunshine Laws for Candidates and Public Officials

In Georgia there are rules restricting conversations between county commissions members when they might meet one another on the street or in a gathering outside official government meetings. There are some similar provisions that apply to those in the judicial arena. I suggest simply extending that principle to require all conversations between candidates for office with those who make campaign contributions and keep that prohibition in place once a person is elected to office. It would extend to lobbyists and anyone wanting to influence policy. It would require any conversation to be in a public forum, or in the offices of government, and that the conversations be recorded by video for the internet in addition to a written record. It would apply to department heads and to all government officials who might have an impact on policy. Basically anything that is said would be available for the public to hear and know about. This is meant to apply to conversations that might impact past, current, or future legislation or policies.

It is meant to cut down on influence peddling by lobbyists, special interest groups, and rich individuals who would use campaign contributions to influence a public official's attitude toward a bill. If they have something to say about a bill, it need not be private. Likewise, any correspondence back and forth to constituents, PAC's, etc. should also be part of the public record.

Elections with Free Media Advertising

If you want candidates to consider the rank-and-file voter more by lessening the power of the special interest and the political action committees who are basically buying elections today this would be a way to do it. It centers on giving free airtime to candidates running for office so they will not be beholden to the big money contributors that pay for the media advertising.

First, In the month of May there would be qualifying for office where anyone wanting to seek office could sign up and pay a small registration fee. No signatures should be required. That person, like all others, could do any form of advertising they wish, however, all television stations and cable sites that do any form of advertising at all would be required to put aside time before each election for candidates to run commercials at no cost. That is the condition of having an FCC license and it would apply to internet sites also. The ad schedule would be as follows:

The June Election-

The June election is to narrow the field of candidates to a maximum of ten. Free political advertising would be run for those who wish to use it for political campaigning advertisements during the third and fourth week of May for a June election. For all media that runs any form of advertising there will be free political advertising on every other day, all day, and all night, and on each both Saturday and Sunday in place of the normal advertising. The ads will be of the same frequency and duration as the advertising that is normally run. During the first days of June till the June election, normally the first Tuesday, there shall be only free political advertising. On the ballot there is no mention of political parties nor if a particular candidate is an incumbent or not.

The October Election-

The Second election is a runoff of the top ten candidates, if there are that many, for each office. Everything else is the same as in the previous election. Free political advertising would be run on alternate days in the third and fourth week of September for the October election which will, again, be on the first Tuesday. From October first to the first Tuesday, there will be nothing but political advertising running on television. Any winner will be required to have over 50 percent of the vote. If no candidate reaches that 50 percent then the top two candidates will go on to the November election.

The November Election

The third election is the final election where the top two candidates will run against each other. To inform the public there will be free time available as before, however in addition to running the political advertisements over the three weekends before the election on Friday night, Saturday night, and Sunday night, there will be hour-long debates for all races on the federal, state, and local races. Only in the case of a write-in candidate would there be a run-off to be held two weeks later.

Under this system candidates like Green Party candidate, Jill Stein, would get some exposure through these free political ads where, as of now (5/2024), she cannot seem to get any coverage even when she was arrested during a protest.

Term Limits

For those who like term limits the members of the congress could have term limits consisting of three terms for a senator and five terms for a member of the house of Representatives. No elected official should directly or indirectly financially benefit from public service or make money from book writing, speaking fees, or lobby activity based on their public service for five years after they leave office.

Chapter 13 - Developing a Block of Voters

The Bernie Sanders and the Ross Perot campaigns in the 1990's show that individuals working together can make an impact into the political process but you must have specific goals and plans to achieve anything real. Also, it must be recognized that Donald Trump has been successful in virtually taking over the Republican Party. It takes surprisingly few people to impact the political process. A national effort can be made with as little as 50 active members in each state. That would be a group of over two thousand members nationwide. I do notice that all these movements, if that is what they were, do have a central figure that people were able to coalesce around but they all had a set of issues too. I like having the focus on the issues with personalities as secondary.

Millenium3 - A Progressive Movement

The terms 'liberal' and 'conservative' have high negatives and being solely in one camp or the other is like putting a target on your back. It is easier to win people over with something fresh and new. "Progressive' is at least descriptive and having a group identifier like "Millennium Three" meaning proposals for humans in the third millennium of history. Supporters can say they are members of the "M3" or be "M3ers." The upshot is that people will not be able to immediately put you or your ideas into a traditional political box and they cannot take shots at you till they first know what you are about.

The collection of proposals in this book are mostly progressive but there are several that are important to conservatives, too. The proposals to not raise taxes on workers should have appeal and limiting the total tax liability to a maximum of 35 percent of a person's income is better than what we have now. The flat tax also has appeal to conservatives and to those who do not fit into any category.

This diversity might not get you as much support as it will keep the criticisms from piling up so fast that people dismiss the proposals out of hand before they can see you are trying to help them. Establishment figures can either embrace you or make life difficult as new ideas might leave them behind. Then there are those who are always afraid of the new and unknown.

I'd focus on how fair these proposals are to all citizens, how they will make life better, and how these things are an eventuality so let's go ahead and move toward them. It's the new world people have been waiting for. Here is a summary of the 'Millennium3 Package proposed in this book:

Universal healthcare
Work partnerships and local partial ownership
Mortgage and credit card caps
A traditional work week
An Updated Voting System
Reinstate the Fairness Doctrine for Media News
Extended Sunshine Laws
A Flat Income Tax
A Taxation Freeze and Income Caps
Wall Street Tax for School Tuition
Term Limits for Federal Offices … and more.

Citizen Apathy

There is little question that the American government does not work in the interests of the average citizen. The average citizen knows this, has always known this, and accepts this as it is all they have ever experienced. The political and economic system walks a fine line where many people are not happy but they are not mad to do anything about it. Perhaps those who are struggling feel they have no time for such activities.

If average citizens could be specific in what they expected from the government and demand it, it would overpower the special interests and paid lobbyists. Right now, they just do not feel like they are being heard.

There are several ways to have a more direct effect on the political agenda. There are several proposals in this book that should make individual participation in political activity more worthwhile. It will at least give people more reason to vote as they will have more to choose from.

We must have a political agenda that will make a difference in the lives of average citizens, not what the establishment tells us is important. The government is not there only to serve the interests of business and those with money. We simply need to address public problems without trying to see if it fits into some political filter, philosophy, or ideology of what government is supposed to be.

Increasing Voting

Not enough people vote in this country. Perhaps they feel it would not change anything. I cannot argue with that as a complaint but people need to vote. I have offered several proposals to make voting more meaningful by making government officials more responsive to the people. However, one step further is to simply offer incentives to increase the number of people voting. We as a people and the government might do the simple thing of offering a tax incentive, perhaps $50.00 per person, to vote or even more direct would be to join the 22 other countries that require all adult citizens to vote. I do think, without any proof to verify it, that if everyone voted it would result in better government.

A Government Website for Gauging Public Opinion

One way to let the government know what average citizens think and feel is to ask them. There is no better way to do this than to establish an official website for that purpose. Each citizen can have input and rank issues based on public expenditures, government actions, and new and proposed laws. There can also be a section for citizens to bring up a new issue and if other people 'like' or 'up vote' that issue to where it reaches a stated threshold that issue would be added to the public discussion.

The survey would alert the government when they take unpopular actions and give the government a 'pulse of the people' on an ongoing basis. When issues have a consistent support of something like 80 percent of the public the government would do well to take notice and the public would do well to wonder why if the government does not. Along with gauging the public interest it could also report on campaign contributions and who the contributors were and other pertinent information in public affairs. There are ways to ensure that each person is only able to have input or vote under one identifier.

Questionnaire on the IRS Form

Another measure to gauge public interest and concerns would be to simply ask them when they file taxes: "How would you like your money spent." It would not be binding, I suppose, but it would give the government an idea how the people funding the government felt about where the money was going. It could gauge support for wars and conflicts, education, welfare, and so on. Government is one of the few entities left that do not ask me how I felt they were doing. I get that opportunity from places like restaurants to doctors' offices to those who provide utility services. Government should update itself and get into the modern world.

Part 4 - Tier Two Domestic Issues

Chapter 14- Backing American Citizens

Among higher income Americans renting apartments and townhouses goes on smoothly enough. However struggling Americans who have fewer resources and often have fewer skills in obtaining and keeping livable rental shelter have difficulties. In every region of America there is substandard rental housing. Low-income renters are in no financial position to forgo substandard housing and the government most often does not require housing to be livable. There should be a national minimum for renting housing so that no American lives in a substandard shelter. To protect the interests of the landlord the government should also hold tenants liable and culpable for any damages beyond normal wear and tear. In the richest country in the world, tenants should not be removed for nonpayment but should draw from a fund that would pay the landlord a partial month's rent when the tenant falls behind. The government could then immediately investigate the cause and help tenants find a job or put them to work in 'workfare' before allowing an eviction. In all cases the tenant would repay housing damages.

Communication Providers

Cable entertainment and phone service providers hook up a digital signal to your home, yet they want to charge double what the government charges to deliver clean drinking water. Yet, we have become so dependent on entertainment and willing to pay for it we pay more for it than we do for natural gas to be piped into our home or electricity to be supplied to our house. It is far simpler to supply the digital signal than of these other utilities and it is much less vital. We all want to be connected to the world and cable television is the primary way of doing it and they offer movies and programming that entertain us. However, let us be real. Many of the movies in the lineup packages are twenty years old and while there are dozens of movie channels often the same movies run on one channel one day and on another the week afterward.

Movie channels have developed a system where they run fewer commercials at the beginning of the movie and then once you're invested to see the end they increase the number and time of the commercial breaks. I have tabulated that in the second half of the movie there may be six minutes of movie time and then as many as fourteen commercials taking up five minutes of time. Plus it is often the same commercial over and over each time there is a commercial break. It cries out for regulation limiting the number of breaks and the time of the breaks. Currently some two-hour movies last three hours and more. Ten minutes of every hour is surely enough commercial interruption.

In the days of antennas we all understood that that TV service was free if we would buy the television and antenna. The programming was paid for by the advertisers who wanted to get exposure to their product. Now it has evolved into a 'have to' service where we are supposed to be willing to pay to get the cable or broadband into our home each month and still we have to watch the commercials. The industry is getting paid twice. Either bill us for the cable and give viewers programming without commercials or stop charging for the service and we will have to sit through commercials as the industry can get paid from the advertisers. If it means that movie stars no longer make fifteen million dollars to make a film I can live with that.

Is it Brainwashing?

Many people cannot with withstand the brainwashing Influence from the constant bombardment of advertising.

Traditionally America has opted for the hands-off public policy of 'let the buyer beware' instead of having widespread consumer protections because people have been taught to fear the government having any control over commerce. That has been convenient for commerce on several different fronts. That policy is not producing the safety the American consumers need today when we are inundated with commercials continually on the TV, radio, internet and when we drive down the public streets with billboards everywhere. With enough repetition we will become interested in buying. Marketing is so slick today that what would have been labeled 'brainwashing' fifty years ago is merely commercialism today. If we demanded better we would get it. It is a commentary on our overall public ability to organize and reject these marketing standards. We are simply oversaturated with advertising. Commercials must become more limited to say something like two minutes of commercials at 10 after, 20 after, 40 after and 50 after the hour. Further, commercial should relay facts and data while not making any unsubstantiated claims or falsehoods. In the meantime I am known as the guy who mutes TV commercials even though my friends eventually poke a little fun at me for doing it.

Internet Coverage

Another disappointing fact is the media industry has poor coverage in too much of the country. If you have ever been in these locations you can see a pause or a disconnect when the programming you are trying to watch switches to a commercial as that data comes from somewhere else. The simple solution is to have better bandwidth but if they industry does not want to increase the bandwidth they cannot run advertising as it disrupts viewing. It will encourage the industry to reach full coverage.

Universal Internet

We are to the point where people need access to the internet and to phone service. People like to communicate with one another for social reasons but it is also part of commerce and, as I point out later in this book, we need to have the ability to talk to one another at home and worldwide about the public issues of the day. Even though this technology has been around for decades not all parts of the USA have reliable phone and internet service due to, I suppose, market forces. Many towns (and businesses) offer free internet as part of the service to attract people to come into that part of the city, etc. If they can do that then, as was advocated in the Bernie Sanders campaign of 2020, the country can afford to have universal internet service and I would say phone reception also. The government can own the satellites and provide the basic services for free or a small flat rate and leave the premium services to the private providers. When we want to be able to talk to those overseas in times of international crises we must be able to do so and that means we need the internet and perhaps the phone service too. We cannot ask for this internationally if citizens in our own country do not have phone and data coverage here in America.

Nightly News

Over the years the evening news and news gathering in general has changed. It seems clear the news is driven more by advertising than an effort to inform the public. In exchange for using the airways it has been suggested that all channels offer morning and evening newscasts without commercial interruption and not sponsored by any company other than the network. It is evident that the character of the news has changed as they compete for ratings. The demeanor of many daily news and political news programming often parallel an issue of Entertainment Tonight, but rather than titillation over celebrities' activities, news organizations often spread fear and are alarmism to keep viewers glued to the programming to keep ratings high. Walter Cronkite once advocated that the news should be a separate division of the networks. I agree. There should be a slot open on all networks and all media that wishes to have news broadcast for an independent company to come in and fill that function. It would be self-contained and have a budget of 5 percent of the network where the news is run.

Harvesting Personal Data

As technology advances companies have more ability to harvest personal information. In the beginning it was only that companies might see what we do on Facebook but now they watch us surf the net and put together profiles of us that are bundled and sold and resold to one company after another. I think it is profitable that Facebook, for example, has millions of customers that they can put small billboards in front of to give a company exposure. We need something short of prying into our lives for the privilege of surfing the web, a web that these companies do not own. I used to really like YouTube but they like Facebook and the others, do not produce the content. They just provide the platform. We are the actors and actresses in this play as well as being the audience. It started out pretty good, but it is looking more and more like traditional TV with ads in online movies. I think we can work something else out that is better for the public.

Fairer and Simpler Contracts

Another improvement that will advance society in America is to provide universal consumer contracts to protect consumers from the technical contracts that are forced on the public by many large corporations such as banks and credit card companies, utility, cable, and cell phone contracts, gyms, rentals, and electronics sales, among others. Many other countries already do this. Currently we are powerless as consumers and cannot do anything about these agreements so we simply sign them without reading the details.

Another problem in routine commercial and consumer contracts is that you cannot take anything the real-life person sitting in front of you says about the goods or services they are selling if they have a written contract. In my time, I have been misled by credit card merchant providers, phone service providers, and loan officers. The salesperson may say you can cancel at any time, but if the contract says otherwise you are stuck. Often a contract will state that the terms cannot be amended or modified by any person, even people who work for that company.

Often institutions use their power to make terms that are not equitable to the consumer including forcing consumers to longer terms than desired, non-competitive rates, and too many miscellaneous fees. They like to charge customers to terminate their service when another company comes along that is more competitive. They use introductory "teaser' rates for a few months and then the rates go up appreciably. You are lucky if you have never signed up for a 'free checking account' only to find out later that they started at some point charging fees for a range of things from moving money from one account to another to just a basic fee for having an account.

To protect the consumer we need a uniform and simple contract agreement that spells out the key points of the service and lays out each other's obligations. The form needs to be very simple. There should be no initiation fees and no annual fees. Most services should be month to month. The monthly rate should be stated. Companies may discontinue services if not paid on time but no late fees in cases where they are not out of any material costs. In other words a gas company could seek reimbursement for having to send someone out to turn a valve, but telephone companies, cable providers, cell phone companies and even electricity are metered services. While non-payments are regrettable, it doesn't cost anything for the company to restore service. It is a flip of the button.

Automatically Renewing Contracts

Also, there should be an end to all automatically renewing contracts in consumer agreements as well as home and apartment rentals. This would include having consumers under contract where all the terms are locked in except the price. Businesses then go up on the rate charged somewhere in the contract term. For those who have charges occurring on their debt or credit cards they may not even notice the charges. Businesses should be locked in as well as the consumer in a more balanced interest between consumers and business.

A Licensed and Accredited Workforce

Here is something that may not be universally popular with the working people I am trying to help because it places an extra burden on them to protect consumers. The problem is that too often construction, manufacturing, along with auto and general repair are done in an unprofessional manner. Car repair and home repair are key areas, for example, where the public has the impression they can be taken advantage of. We know the problem, which is some repairmen have learned the trade from their elders or are learning the trade as they go. Having some formal education may or may not have been part of that process. I suggest that these industries have some combination of formal training, that technicians and workers have certifications, and that they document their work at every stage. Currently some states have fairly good laws on the book to try and protect consumers while other states seem to side with the businesses and leave the consumer on their own. We need a uniform code of protection across the country. All work should come with an estimate of costs and inform the consumer when and if they exceed the estimate. The work should be photographed and documented so it can be shown that not only was the work truly performed but done in a manner that can be checked on later. Labor rates should be inline with labor rate hours established by the government. In car work, replaced parts should always be returned to the consumer.

It may be that there will be a tiered pricing system where service providers and laborers with certifications can charge according to a standard rate but those without certifications must charge less.

A Bureau of Standardization and Simplification

I grew up in workshop, literally. I began holding the light for my dad when I was 12 and I was all but running a small sport car repair by the time I was 16. I've worked on all aspects of cars, boats, and house construction. When computers came along I began by selling them and then building them for sale. In all this I have learned that often the different manufacturers used different screws to hold on similar sheet metal. Why force us to have two different skews when one size would serve for both applications. The same principle applies from everything from plugs to the color codes of wires.

Also the thousands of working people who visit the nationwide automobile parts stores must endure all kinds of frustrations to do repairs made more difficult through either poor design or a neglect of the mass auto manufacturers to think of how difficult it will be to repair them.

I suggest that the public request products be made simpler, with more standardization, and more repairable for the end user. A progressive government consumer agency would be able to put such ideals into realities.

Manufacturers Warranties

How many times have we come across what many consider lemons in, say, the automobile industry as just one example. A particular car model or drivetrain part just doesn't hold up. Often there are recalls fixing some problems but often there are not. The same can be said to happen in consumer electronics, smart phones, and to clothing that doesn't hold their shape or color. No one wants to bankrupt these companies by over burdening them with recalls, but when they make windfall profits and have executives making tens of millions of dollars per year we should hold their products to a high standard.

In recent decades Americans have been content to have less quality to have a lower price. That is different than what was the norm when I was young. To verify this just look at the complexity of an IBM typewriter in the old days and look at a current computer keyboard now. There is a world of difference. Somewhere in the middle would be more acceptable. We need enough quality to assure that the product works and has enough serviceability that we are not constantly replacing those products.

Product Performance and Customer Satisfaction

Regarding products made by major manufacturers that are essential to living we need to be assured the products are being improved each year to improve quality, simplicity, reliability as well as price along with other aspects like safety. When a problem appears we need a system for collecting data on the perform products and putting them into a data base so it is clear there is a problem and force the manufacturers to make the needed changes.

The Lottery

Both Geroge Washington and Thomas Jefferson were said

to have sponsored a lottery for their benefit in their lifetimes. Recently, states have approved lotteries and it was started to help fund schools. More states have signed on to various lottery systems and it has ballooned somewhat with more gambling offerings. I'm not a great fan of gambling, but if we are to have a lottery I would prefer to have the winning number be one of the tickets sold not a magic number that may or may not be on any printed ticket. It makes the odds much lower that a winning number will be selected. I think there should be a winner each time the drawing is held and that is the way to do it. It would have smaller payouts but the lottery would have a winner for each drawing.

Gambling

Gambling has always been with us and in my lifetime it has been made more legitimate in the US. Nothing of value is made or produced in gambling and it flies in the face of math and reason. It falls more into the area of temptation and desperation. However, I have a few friends who gamble and can afford the small losses they incur while on vacation. However, on my two trips to a casino I saw people who were not there as part of a vacation but there to try win big to change their lives. Most of them will be disappointed. The overwhelming odds are that you will lose more than you gain. It is a way of taking money from people and giving nothing back. I would not want to make money that way and I consider it only one step from criminal activity. My concern is that people gamble money they need for other things. About 15 percent of the participants win in organized casino gambling with most winners receiving a small sum of money. The overwhelming remaining participants lose money. Casino gambling in the USA reaches into the hundreds of billions of dollars annually.

Since a court decision in 2018 sports gambling has come to America legally. Americans spend over 100 billion dollars on sports betting with one site reporting over 250 billion dollars projected for 2024. The odds of losing, according to studies, is from 60 to 80 percent depending on the study with 20 percent of those losing money that was needed for necessities. It is simply not the way to build a successful society.

One aspect of gambling I would put into law is that no gambling debt can be legally collected on. Payment is fully voluntary. That might limit gambling to prepaid ticket purchase and the like. Few would be extending credit collection on any bad debt was unenforceable.

A Food Rating

Most of us are aware that Americans consume less healthy food than desirable. We eat more often for taste than nutrition. Over the last century the nutrition label system has made some improvements in our food system listing the freshness date, the ingredients list, and a nutrition breakdown. However, it has not been enough to change the dietary habits of many people. What would be more effective is to have a label on the front with a simple code for food that is heathy or not healthy as it is related to maintaining the human body. To make it more palatable (no pun intended) to both consumers and producers is to have a numerical code from 1 to 5. One is healthy, three are occasionally OK to consume, and 5 is simply not healthy. It could come with an explanation underneath the number or offer an extensive explanation online at the FDA website. It would be hard to do in today's climate where the public has little power and the special interest has great power. That is why we need to change the system. We need a system that promotes the health of citizens and not just serve the organized special interest who have money at stake in the arrangement.

Chapter 15 Welfare

In the 1960's President Lyndon Johnson was able to get

landmark legislation passed that was touted to end poverty in this country. While that has not happened, the poverty rate has fallen from 26 percent back in the early 1960's to around 15 percent today. When Ronald Reagan came into power he painted a picture of 'welfare queens' lying around in government supported housing watching reruns on a big screen TV all day. After welfare reforms in the 1990's the welfare rolls have been cut in half. Sixty percent of all those single moms out there who are getting assistance also work and there are limits on how long anyone can get welfare. In some states there is a three-year limit on welfare. Still people remember the Reagan era images of unmarried women in the ghettos with large screen televisions in government supported housing while next door abled body men are laying on the couch watching daytime reruns while the American taxpayer works full time just to make it to the next paycheck. That imagery has elected many Republicans, particularly at the state level.

Poverty programs are not there because the poor outvoted others. If the facts mean anything, the poor people do not vote in vast numbers. The poor vote in lower numbers than any other economic class of America. They are not controlling the elections. The poor split their vote by supporting Democrats about two to one. While this is a clear division in favor of the Democratic Party, the Republicans are getting a good portion of the vote.

Workfare in America

At one time there was a call for a more efficient way to battle poverty in this country, one that would move people out of poverty more directly and one that would appease critics of the 'transfer payments' system as they saw it. Those taxpayers are tired of paying taxes and watching people in the grocery stores buy inefficient food items and 'paying' for them with food stamps and now food cards. It may be an exaggeration, but more Americans are feeling that there is a permanent welfare state and they are tired of paying for it. It is not an unmanageable problem with less than fifteen percent of families living within the poverty level, but it is certainly enough to take a new course of action to reduce that to under five percent. If we do nothing we continue a system that has little chance of changing the poverty rate in this country. We will still have a higher poverty rate than Russia, our old allies in the United Kingdom, and our neighbors in Canada, along with three dozen other countries big and small all over the globe.

Along with building highways and defending the country, the government is also responsible for addressing the issues that arise when a portion of the public is not able or has not elected to take part in the economic system used by the whole. The world's richest nation should not turn its back on the unemployed and those who are in poverty. Second, if we did turn our back it would result in chaos and social disruption that would in the end be more expensive. To whatever extent able bodied adults are on welfare, about one percent, the most practical option is to take the money that is being spent toward welfare and put them into more productive workfare programs.

There are few problems that could not be helped by a good job that enables people to make a living and be able to pay their routine bills. Next, is that feeling of being lost that people get when they are left behind and they feel they do not have anything fulfilling in their life. The working people of this country should have some assurance that the tax money they give over to the community chest is not being taken from the working and given to those who could work but are not. Making a world where people feel they have something invested in the community like a good job and a good life is probably the best hedge against uncivilized behavior.

There are several approaches that could be taken including developing an improved system of government employment offices nationwide that are expanded to include training and teaching skills to new workers who cannot find jobs and have no prospects. They can take on young workers who have no training or experience. Additionally, let's be sure people can get any and all training available to prepare them for work. That includes a college education, but one geared toward improving the person in a measurable way to either make them a better citizen or get them a better job. But let us not pay people to use school to put off having to work.

The public might embrace a system where tax money is converted from welfare to workfare. In this system the welfare money is paid to the recipient, but they are being paid to show up at a potential employer who had agreed to try them out in a job. In essence the employer gets to try the employee out for thirty to ninety days to see if it would benefit the company by hiring this individual. If it turns out to be useful the employers would have to take over the payments. If it doesn't work out, the taxpayer has not really spent any more money than they were spending before and the recipient has had to work to receive the money.

In the Roosevelt years there was a public works program. They are best remembered for public works projects, repairing roads, and building parks. Today, while a number of projects could be considered, teaching the unemployed construction skills would have long term benefits. It is productive work, the country always needs new structures in times of prosperity, and it is one area where foreign labor cannot take away jobs from American workers because the work must be done on site. One of the projects they could undertake is to build public housing for welfare recipients who are already getting housing assistance. Then those recipients could begin to pay for the housing as they would be employed building units to live in. They could restore older structures and restore the homes of retired people who have worked all their lives but now cannot maintain their homes due to age. Again, it is not as if the taxpayer would be spending any more money. It is that the taxpayer would be requiring something in return for the assistance check.

Chapter 16 - A Revolution in Education

America is in a good position to show its leadership in the world again by updating the traditional methods of education. With our creativity we are well suited to update or supplement the traditional teacher in front of the classroom and revamp the lecture method of teaching which has been in place for centuries.

Rather than continuing to pay ten times the fair market price for hardback books, we could replace them with online instructional and learning videos that are ten times more effective and fifty times less in costs at every level in education from kindergarten to PhD programs. You can already see some of these cropping up on learning channels on television and the internet too. If done well a set of videos would do for each subject and they could be used across the nation and beyond.

Where traditional lectures are used in the classroom they could be videoed and placed on the internet so that students could review it later. This is harder for teachers as they will be 'on camera' but before long all the videos will become commonplace and teachers will get used to doing them. If a particular teacher could just not bring themselves to be on camera or felt their presentation was off on a particular day, they could select the best lectures from other schools that covered that material. As time went on there would be a complete set of quality lectures on each chapter that could be viewed by anyone. On any day, the teacher might choose to show one of those videos rather than teach so students would have access to lectures that had received high ratings for clarity and comprehension. Then the teacher could go over the salient points and bring the class into a discussion of the material they just watched.

With a classroom of networked computers at each student's deck the teacher can go over material and then allow the student to answer a list of questions that will show which student understood the lesson and which didn't. This is not to grade the student nor stand over them, but to help them learn. This approach is in use in places today. A classroom might show the interactive 3D learning video on Monday, a lecture taken from a famous university on Tuesday with a computer review on Thursday and Friday to help students in the areas the computer shows they have not mastered the work.

Next, the educational system must lower the pressure on students so they will not be burned out on learning. Abroad test scores are higher because they have greater incentive to get ahead and see learning as the path. There is little other option for them. In America there are many other things to compete for the attention of the student. That is a big part of why we are losing many of our students and it is why people do not make a lifetime of learning. Students are all too often burned out on learning and many do not see how the material they cover benefits them in everyday living. Schools need to make a connection from learning to daily life and reinforce the value of learning.

Are Children Ready and Able to Learn?

All the technology and modernization in the world will not help if the student doesn't come to school ready to learn or does not want to learn. It is in society's interest to reach the troubled students and help them when they have problems at home or at school that prevents them from benefiting from the educational opportunities the taxpayers seek to provide for them. Otherwise, what is the point? It will just cost taxpayers more down the road. Fix the problems while they are young. It will take more social workers, with more skills and more scope, but it is a practical way to save tax money overall. Finding the obstacles to learning is the key to increasing the percentage of successful students in the future.

Maybe there is a problem at home, a problem with diet, sleep etc. as to why a young student cannot concentrate on the subject matter. In many areas in the country students fall behind in learning more than in the rest of the nation and there must be reasons for this and where a student is not doing well it would be ideal to find out why.

Are there problems at home that, for whatever reason, keep the child from coming to school rested, well clothed, and well fed? Are there problems at home that make the children's mental state upset where they are distracted to the point that it interferes with their ability to learn? Are the social influences around them distracting to the student? Are they spending too much time with television or TikTok etc. or too much time unattended?

Does the student have the ability to focus on the teacher or subject matter without mentally drifting away? If a student cannot focus, despite personal ambition to succeed it is more of a mountain to climb. Maybe they are just geared differently and we generally penalize those students with failing grades although they have tried more than what should be expected of them in terms of time and effort. The next area is the question of learning ability or the ability and willingness to absorb material.

Are they not able to interact with other students and is that disability causing them to lose interest in learning? Are they easily frustrated, do they turn that frustration into anger, depression, or some other state that prevents learning and social growth?

Is it a problem of habit, discipline, or is the subject matter not presented as relevant or interesting? These are among the things administrators and parents must consider retaining students and maximize the learning experience for them. In some instances the subject matter may need to be presented in a way that is more interesting to the students and where they can see that it relates to everyday life or to occupational work. It doesn't hurt to keep reinforcing why the tasks they perform are beneficial. If teachers cannot defend the subject matter then it is no surprise students might lose interest in learning too much of it. Perhaps some students are inundated with too much information and asked to absorb it too quickly only to recite some of it for an exam then they discard the information.

Some students are sent home with complex homework and term projects that conflict with what they wish was their private time. Their parents work at a job and when they come home they do not generally bring their work home with them. Students do and students are not paid to go to school. Why would, say, high school students in a poor community with little prospects for a dreamy life after graduation want to invest this kind of time when there are more pleasurable things to do? They really want some time to escape from the school routine but they do the homework because they are forced to do it.

Again, public education is working for some students, maybe a majority, but the local high school in my area had a twenty-five percent dropout rate. That is a big percentage of the community to write off and among the more successful students you will find the rate of burn-out is high.

Maybe making learning more relevant will help. At some point the public has a vested interest in having the student learn the practical aspects of how to live independently. That would include learning what it takes to pay bills, get a job, run a home etc. It would need to include the expenses of car ownership including insurance and repairs. It would also cover how much it costs to have a child and how much of a lifestyle change it is to raise them.

At the higher level, it is hard to convince a struggling college student who must work to support themselves to spend money to go to school and be required to take literature classes when what they want is job training. They just can't make the connection and the subjects do not interest them.

In some cases the curriculum may be suspect, in some it is in elements of home life. In other cases it may take a psychologist to work with individuals or with groups of individuals to sort out learning problems to improve the overall student and youth experience. These are things that we can do and more if we merely choose to do them

Group of Five

The 'Group of five' is a concept to prevent young children from being left out of the social mix for whatever reason in elementary school classrooms. Sometimes isolation is just a temporary thing; sometimes it is permanent or long term and sets the stage for a lifetime of disconnection from people. This is not healthy for the child and it is not healthy for society as too often loners and people who are disconnected are more inclined to do activities that harm society. It is a program that doesn't cost anything. In essence, it is somewhat like the swim instructor assigning a swim partner when first going into the pool. The instructor wants to have an extra assurance that no one drowns when they may be looking away. It is the same concept, but instead of a concern for actual drowning it is a social concern and all that goes with it. It might start by having tasks to share like being sure everyone understands the class work or homework assignment or to help each other as a team. It must include the social component as the point is for children to help each other and to have a system for doing it. When something is amiss it is structured so that any one of the five members of a group can go to the teacher with a concern when the group or a member runs into a situation that is not being resolved. Once the system is underway it could be applied throughout school and perhaps even in the workplace later in life. In the end, every person would benefit from being in at least one safety group somewhere be it at work, club, or in their professional and recreational groups..

Peace and Progress Software for School

Since the 1990's I have wanted a software program or field of study among school children to develop their knowledge of world affairs, look at world problems, and put forth what they thought would be solutions to them. It might be in the form of an online program, software like Sim City for world problems, or an annual class project. If it started at some point in elementary school and went through high school the students would not only have a good working knowledge of world affairs but would most likely have some workable solutions. Perhaps if it continued in college there could be a comparison among the different schools' proposals for the most workable solutions.

Life Planning Software

Another software I have thought beneficial for children is a life planning program for students to list what occupations they think would interest them when they grow up. It could also cover a list of areas from where they think they would like to live, what hobbies they might enjoy and how they would pay for those things. I would keep it easy and fun but as the years progressed they would benefit from having thought about the future before they graduate.

Chapter 17- Crime and Punishment

A New Police Force

Before we can even discuss crime and punishment, we should discuss the recurring development of police officers abusing their authority in making arrests. In several of these videos the suspects were beaten and even killed. We might develop a totally new approach on how the police react in these situations. First having two officers in each police car would mean a police officer would always have a backup when they approach a suspect. Secondly, it must be understood that suspects should not argue with police officers. If they are innocent, it will come to light. However, when a suspect is belligerent, rather than 'taking them down' by force, why could it not be understood that belligerent suspects are free to walk to the patrol car and voluntarily get into the back seat. Then at the police station, there would be time and people better suited to handle the situation. That would include a suspect representative. If necessary, we could more easily redesign the back seats of police vehicles cheaper than the nation could withstand the uproar of seeing suspects being abused. Perhaps when people are brought into the police station for booking the desk sergeant or booking officer could be empowered to decide to either dismiss a nuisance charge right there or write out a citation for a court date without putting them in jail for minor infractions. At any rate, these occurrences have been going on long enough that change must occur on both sides. If a suspect will not walk toward the vehicle then the officers should have a unit they can call that is trained to handle those types of situations. A sort of negotiator for those types of arrests.

In a 2022 incident a youth ran through a police routine safety stop and was shot 60 times after a high-speed car chase. He was unarmed. First, I see no reason to run through a safety stop. But I do wonder what would happen if the police merely recorded the vehicle tag and over the next few days the owner could be located and questioned. This is particularly true if the police were not on the lookout for anyone. This a conjecture but no one would have died in a middle of the night shooting and travelers on the highways would not have been put at further risk from a high-speed chase.

In more than a few of these tragedies it involved an inflamed circumstance where the suspect does not comply with the police. All citizens need to comply with the police. The question for society is whether the penalty for disobedience death is.

Incarceration

America has a lot of people in prison. We have mandatory minimum sentences that assure America will put people in prison at high rates. We have more people in prison in America than they have in prison in communist China, a place not known for civil liberties. It is a result of candidates running for office declaring they will not be soft on crime. When they are elected they pass laws that ratchet up sentences where people can be incarcerated for ten years for a small amount of cocaine and for more years than they used to get for committing murder.

A majority of these incarcerated people are poor. These people have broken away from society and there must be a reason for this. The number one reason is, by and large, they have an insufficient stake in society so they do not go along. It would be cheaper to fix the problem on the front end rather than have the greater costs later. The cost to society is many more times the cost of job training and other forms of assistance in getting people employed. There is the cost of the police to monitor the community and catch criminals. Then there is the cost of the judicial setting and the trials. Then there is the cost of housing them for the years they are behind bars. It has been said we could send prisoners to Harvard cheaper than we could keep them in prison.

A New Prison System

If we want to reduce crime, reduce the tax burden required to chase criminals, and the cost of keeping them housed away from society we should look towards the reasons for crime. When they have failed society and are in prison we should teach them life improvement skills, social skills, and how to stay away from things that might tempt them toward crime when they are released. Their environment, their social and economic status, and having no direction or goals are surely factors when people drift away from civility. Loneliness and a lack of social connections may also figure into a disaffection from social norms. It is imperative that we have programs in the prison system to help them rejoin our productive society.

Most of the crime in the US could be put into two categories: income related and drug related crime. Anyone who is arrested for drug related crimes or where it is shown they have committed crime to buy drugs should undergo drug addiction classes. It is in our interest to find out why they got on drugs in the first place. Then they can undergo classes to give them some tools to stay off drugs and stay away from the factors that trigger drug use. No one should go to prison with just a sentence of time. If they are to return to society they need more than a grown-up version of 'time-out.'

Along with the prescribed time for each prisoner's incarceration for a crime against the peace and tranquility of society, they should be rehabilitated and understand why criminal activity is wrong. They should understand why it is counterproductive and have a full understanding of the proper workings of a civil society. They need to be able to verbalize why society needs rules and why they should be followed, why rules are just, and how to get along within those rules. There should be requirements of learning and indoctrination so they would have the tools and skills needed to succeed in society.

This includes social skills of communication and appearance as well as technical skills. Among the things I would require is that they learn to be presentable in appearance, learn to speak well, learn good manners, and learn polite conversation. These things would be done to help the prisoner and give society the best shot at having a productive citizen. It is not meant to be further punishment; it is more like catching them up on things they missed when growing up for whatever reason.

Many prisoners are repeat customers. We should do all we can to see that society does not go through the expense of having prisoners repeatedly break the law and repeatedly force society to put them away. Each prisoner should learn how to read and write and should write a short paper each week. It teaches them mental organization and verifies what they are reading. Perhaps there are specific things that should be included in the readings. If a person has broken into a liquor store and shot someone they should read about the tragedy of families who have lost someone to shootings.

What we need to recognize is that prisoners who are going to be released back into society need the positive socialization they obviously missed the first time. Most of us had many positive influences on us such as parents, churches, schools, etc. Apparently, it was not enough for these people and so more effort will have to go into it than with the general population.

The biggest problem in this country and probably across the world is having nothing productive to do. It leads to more crime, drug use and more mischief than anything else. Whatever is happening (or not happening) on the street is what we need to focus on if we want less crime. We will need to replace selling drugs and similar criminal activities with legitimate opportunities.

If people in prison are learning from others about crime, then I would not allow prisoners to talk to each other until they have gone through training and education. I would not allow them to talk about the 'old days.' Swapping 'war stories' and exchanging ideas on how to be more successful in crime is not helpful.

In place of cable television I would air educational programming and a series of programs on learning civilized skills. Later prisoners could watch the news and make a report about the programs they watch and take turns giving a report to a group of the prisoners, kind of like speech class. The television news usually covers a section of political, economics, sports, and other current events of the day. Prisoners could report on that for practice. Before they would be eligible to be released they would need to be able to do college level presentations.

A basic education for all people in prison, in jail, and on assistance, should be available. Some programs will need to be patterned to fit their special needs but the remainder could come from the classes springing up on the internet. Prisons would become places to learn as well as for incarceration. I am sure there are people better qualified to develop specific classes, but something along these lines appears reasonable:

101- Civics including the common good, common benefit, golden rule including why we should be peaceful and not steal from others, etc.
102- Why we have a government, how it works, what it costs, how we pay for it and the benefits of it. It would include public services, police, and the court system, among other areas.
103- Reading, writing, practical math, and basic science.
104- What it costs to live independently. How to do a home budget, what it costs to rent or own a home or apartment along with car costs, food, and clothing costs.
105- Having children. A close look at what is involved in raising children including the time, effort, and costs that go into the pleasures and responsibilities of having children.
106- How to make a living. How to select a skill or trade.
107- How to prepare for work and have a routine and plan for the work cycle.
108- Learning a skill to make a living.

109- How to present yourself to others. How to dress for the public and how to communicate in public and interface with others.
110- General hygiene. How to bathe, groom yourself, and maintain general health.
111- The social structure. The family, what it is and how it works. How to make friendships and have companions. Why people join groups such as community, social, and even political groups?
112- Diet. Food consumption and food buying.
113- Finding the motivation to work and live in the modern world.
114- Mental attitude. How to maintain a peaceful demeanor. How to handle anger etc.

By the time they are ready to go back into society they will be easily noticed for their good manners and good presentation. They would have one or more skills in which they excelled so if someone would take a chance on hiring a person that had been in prison they would be getting a very well-trained employee

Sexual Assaults in Prisons

Last, I want to mention the reflection in movies and public opinion about forced sex in prison. I do not know if it happens or not. It is unclear reading about it on the internet. There are isolated cases discussed, but does it happen routinely? If it does occur it should be stopped. That is cruel and unusual punishment and it is wrong on many levels. That so many people seem to not only accept this notion but think it acceptable leaves me wondering what kind of people have we become? We cannot claim to be a nation of civilized people when citizens allow others to be treated in that manner.

Decriminalizing Drug Use

We spend too much time and resources arresting otherwise harmless citizens and processing them through the jail, court, and prison system. We notice that most of the citizens that go to prison are poor and most are black although drug use seems to occur throughout the entire population. It is an addiction and a weakness more than a crime.

While I do not care for the legal use of recreational drugs within our society, there are many other people with other views. Since I first wrote about this, many states have made marijuana legal to possess in small quantities. In Tennyson's 'The Lotus Eaters' the crops are in the field and the village is in decay as they have only one interest (to consume the Lotus) and that is my prime concern about drugs. We surmise that many young people try drugs at a certain age for a variety of reasons. Perhaps it is peer pressure, perhaps they cannot make it in other activities so they can hide behind the good feeling of drugs and find friends who are sharing their dysfunction. Maybe they are escaping from the thoughts of facing up to social conventions and adult responsibility. Maybe drug use is among their first decisions without their parents' help or oversight and they simply make poor decisions. They may just find it fun or they are simply bored. Maybe it is a coming-of-age experience. Drugs are a place to go and hide or to retreat, but in the end they are an illusion. Do we find our existence so frightening, boring, full of toil or oppression that drugs are needed as an escape from it?

I do think we need to remove the commercial promotion of all vices. We should put forth the effort to convince the young people of tomorrow that drug use and partying is not the object of society. It is a bit harder if their parents do the same thing, but with alcohol instead of drugs. When we think of the world we want to have, is it one where our people are on drugs? What is wrong with our world that we cannot have fun being normal?

Drugs and Violence

South of the border, when a drug crop can be grown for a dollar and sold for $300.00 it creates a scenario where people with no other way to survive will apparently murder without hesitation in the drug related crime business. There are ruthless people in the drug trade. It would help if there were some alternatives to growing and selling drugs in these poor countries where it is about the only growth industry they have. Helping people plan for a better society down in the drug torn countries will help us in the long run. There are programs in place now but they are not stopping the flow of drugs. Without the programs, though, it would be worse.

Those making a three hundred to one profit will not stop until made to do so. We should work both ends of the street by finding an alternative to growing drugs and reducing the profit they can get for the drugs. Uruguay is legalizing marijuana to see if they can reduce the violence. It will be interesting to see how this experiment works. Now several states in America have joined in legalizing marijuana,. We will see what results.

Although drug use has tapered off to a stable level in this country over the last years, I would still do whatever it takes to end drug trafficking from other countries. The entire process from the time crops are grown in other countries until it reaches the American streets is laden with crime and death. In Mexico it is said that 60,000 people have been killed over drug related crime. In South America, another 20,000 can be put on that list. It takes over some towns south of the border and that violence surely spills over into America. I suspect that the drug smugglers have more money to spend than the government because the markup is high on drugs and that big money causes them to be willing to do any level of violence. Most political figures are afraid to take on the drug problem out of personal fear.

Removing the criminal penalties for growing some drugs here in America and allowing them to be sold without advertising and promotion might reduce the importation from other countries. People say the process of decriminalizing these vices will not increase the number of people using them; here some general guidelines that seem to be what people have in mind:

Marijuana. $250.00 fine and require they only drive to work and home for ninety days. No drug use during this time. After three tickets you must attend life planning and substance abuse classes.

Cocaine. $2,500.00 fine, only allow going from work to home for ninety days. No use at home or have any drugs on their property. Users must attend life planning and substance abuse classes. On the second arrest comes a sentence of 30 days in jail, then 90, then six months in jail. Each time they must complete the classes and pay the fines.

Marijuana may be grown if registered and sold at a government set price. People may only have it in their homes and on private property. Since I wrote this Colorado and other states have legalized recreational pot use. Several other states have followed. We will see how it goes.

The DUI

Most of us have personal knowledge of someone they know that has been harmed by a drunk driver or knows someone who has a drinking problem. In having a DUI, it is not that people cannot drive; it is that they cannot drink and drive safely. However, when caught, society does not limit their ability to drink; we limit their ability to drive. However, once someone drinks they are less rational and might drive anyway. The answer, to me, is to focus on limiting people who cannot drink from drinking in public. That could easily be accomplished by punching a hole in their driver's license (indicating they had a DUI). A bartender or cashier at a convenience store would simply ask to see the driver's license of people purchasing alcohol. While people might be able to get around this, it would curtail most of the undesirable activity.

The criticism of this plan is that many drinkers do not want to be bothered by being required to show their license. It is too much of an inconvenience, although some large chain stores require anyone buying alcohol to show a license no matter what their age as some restaurants do to lessen the liability of being caught selling to an underage person. To encourage others from buying alcohol for someone who is prohibited from drinking in public, society could fine them $1,000.00 and then punch their driver's license too, so they cannot purchase alcohol any longer.

As a society we have come to accept that people wish to drink in public. But when a percentage of those people get behind the wheel of a vehicle after drinking, non-drinking drivers have a right to ask for some form of protection. Arresting drunks after they cause an accident is hardly enough when any bartender or cashier could easily prevent much of it. All it takes to save lives is to show an ID. Placing a small limitation on the alcohol industry would greatly lessen the cost to society as there would be fewer accidents and fewer people harmed by drunk driving. Those people are still free to drink at home and at the homes of other people. And there is not any real cost added to the alcohol industry or to the state, just the cost of making the holes in the licenses. Is a minute of inconvenience to show an ID worth this? My answer is "Yes."

The other provision that would greatly limit public drunkenness would be to hold bars responsible for patrons that drink to the point they become legally intoxicated while being on their property. It would really stress the bar owners, but it would be the right thing to do.

There are other options, too. Breathalyzers packs can cost about ten dollars for a five pack of saliva strips to a professional breathalyzer machine that can cost a thousand dollars. Making these tests available for patrons who drink, or requiring it, could help reduce the 20,000 deaths that occur due to drunk driving each year in the US.

Crime in Relation to Poverty and Drugs

I suspect many of the people in prison for burglary have one thing in common in that they are below the poverty line, they have no money in the bank, they have little ability to make money, few job skills, and have little assets to lose if they are caught and imprisoned. If they had assets they value or had a legitimate way to make money it might make a difference. A significant number of the people in jail are there for a drug related crime. For hard drug users, it might be better to offer free substitutes of less addictive and less dangerous drugs. It is cheaper for society and removes the criminal activity in smuggling and street crime. Many drug users commit theft to raise money for drugs. Having stolen items sold in the underground market at ten cents on the dollar to buy drugs could be mostly eliminated through decriminalizing drug use. It would save money now used for law enforcement, the court system expenses, and the incarceration expense. It is not possible to keep determined people from being on drugs by making them illegal. Anti-drug campaigns, commercials, and anti-drug campaigns in schools are probably more effective in addition to removing the root problems for drug-use.

Violence Rating System

How can it be that we see human violence as an acceptable mode of behavior? We do not teach that violence is repugnant in the way we teach other misbehaviors. Perhaps we take it for granted that people innately see it as wrong but unavoidable. Perhaps we have been socialized to see it as the ultimate way to resolving conflicts. In the large scheme of things we see war as the way to resolve conflicts among nations where we could just as easily see it as an unacceptable method. If we rejected human violence we could just put things in place so that wars are simply not possible like eliminating offensive armaments.

It is not healthy or progressive to have a mindset that glorifies war and violence. Removing human violence from our lives might be harder than teaching school children to sit quietly during lectures or teaching drivers to drive on the same side of the road but more effort needs to go into making the transition from Barbarians to civilized human beings. Equality among people is probably the best way to reduce human violence on all levels along with not neglecting those truly in need.

In the meantime we could make notice of our exposure to violence by having a code that applies to our arts and entertainment that is not much different than the one used for sex and language in the movie codes. It would apply to videos, movies, books, etc. that have gratuitous violence unless it reflected reality or historical events. Beyond the media, it could also extend to boxing, football, and other sports as well.

Violence Tax?

In the earlier years I wanted to have a violence tax like a cigarette tax, but that might invite freedom of speech problems. Still, the world has such a backlog of older movies that were made around the time computer animation came into being. Blowing stuff up and shooting a lot of people seemed to be prevalent in these movies. These things are hardly works of art. I don't see they contribute anything to society. They hang out on many of the no cost channels. Are we to have to endure seeing these violent movies for eternity as they are almost freely available as few people want to pay to see them?

Chapter 18- A Hand Up

A Basic Shelter

America is the richest nation to ever be on the earth. The time has come for every person in America who wants to be part of society to have their basic needs met, a shelter to live in, basic healthcare, and a job. If a job cannot be found the government can implement a job training program. Each community can analyze their needs to determine what would be required to enable every citizen in their community to have those basic needs met, the cost, and how they suggest it could best be done. It must include a job plan so people can be self-reliant.

Housing for the Displaced

We have animal shelters for homeless animals. We have places on the side of the road as designated rest areas for travelers on our interstates, but no identical network of shelters for displaced and indigent people. We have advanced too far to allow people to keep living under bridges and in tents in the woods. It still happens in your city, although you may not know about it. Try to imagine a country where there is temporary housing for people who are on their own and having some sort of problem but cannot afford to check into a hotel. In a country as rich as America we should have temporary housing for everyone who needs a place to stay. Once they are there, workers can try to determine whether they need help with personal or social problems or whether it is just economics.

There are about 15 million families in poverty today and that seems like a big number when it is divided into the fifty states with hundreds of communities in each state and you can see it is more manageable, particularly for an abundant country like America. It will take planning and allocating both funds and responsibilities, but it can be done, like many other programs, cost effectively.

A Country with No Dilapidated Housing

In a larger project to spur the economy and to meet the needs of the people I propose a national project to replace every rundown house in America. It would be on the same scope as the mission to put a man on the moon in the 1960's. Where it is desired to save old housing I would update and rebuild only those that were on very solid footing and of a desirable shape, design, and location. There is little advantage in adding new siding to an old home if it has termite damage, on a site that floods, or is too close to its neighbors to be a good location for housing.

We will have armies of workers building houses. It will be greatly made up of the unemployed, students, and people of retirement age who still have a lot to offer the public. People may come and go from this army, but the skills they learn can be used in their own home and as an occupation throughout their life.

This program would transfer people from welfare to workfare and sell the homes back to the crew members who are building them. It will provide new homes and create jobs for planners of new subdivisions to plumbers and electricians along with the skilled and semi-skilled labor force. The modernization into new homes and rebuilt ones will reduce the energy needs. I have seen entire neighborhoods that have mostly run-down housing. Where applicable, I would move everyone to a new location (where new homes have already been built) and I would then tear down the old homes and build new ones in their place.

There would be a litmus test to get into one of these new homes. There is little sense in fixing up homes just to have them torn apart by people who do not take care of their property. Having ownership and the opportunity to have a home should provide enough incentive to keep most of it from happening. I suspect social workers who work in these areas know more about this, but people will need to show they are ready to be responsible citizens.

Cars for $50.00 a Week

A significant problem the young and the poor have is getting back and forth to work. Given the number of cars in this country and the number traded in toward newer models, the government could buy some of the better ones and maintain a fleet of cars and rent them out to the working poor for $50.00 per week if they are working. In addition to providing people with a way to get to work, the cars could be serviced by technical schools, in part or in full, by students who are studying mechanics. The private sector could service them, too, if needed, if they are on the approved list when the schools are overburdened and can bill at a discounted rate using labor rate hours plus parts at ten percent mark-up over wholesale. If the cars are abused the people using the car must come to the shop on their days off and help fix the car as part of their penalty.

Uncle Sam Wants You

Today, some people would like to serve their country or humanity without having to go into combat. These people might consider one of a dozen or so 'civilian' armies. It would be like the military army but for nonviolent purposes. Some could be full-time like the military where they house people and move them around anywhere in the world. Some could be part time and they would return home each evening. It could be a summer job during a school break. In summary here are a few of the areas in which Peace Corp type organizations could be used here in the USA and abroad.

Community Builder Corps

The home building plan would build new housing and build new commercial spaces for people in depressed regions of America. It could be rural or urban. It could also focus on removing slum houses and replacing them or it could refurbish homes of those who are older, disabled, or single parents with children.

International Relief Corps

This would be a multifunctional army of people who might assist relief agencies with the logistics of food, medicine, and other supplies and basically sub-contract under the established relief agencies to assist them in humanitarian efforts abroad. Some might work at domestic warehouses. Where people have specialized skills they might be deployed in the field. This would include medical skills, construction and road building skills, infrastructure skills and those with knowledge on how to place wells and install ground sewerage facilities among other projects.

Environmental Corps

Wherever the water, soil, or air needs monitoring or where there is a program of environmental hazard cleanup, people could be trained and utilized to help promote a greener planet.

Home and Yard Improvement Corps

Another team could clean people's yards, remove eyesores, and help with most home repairs that are causing the home to deteriorate like a leaking roof or missing gutters. This would be aimed at senior citizens, the poor, and those who are disabled.

Family Corps

Wherever a family expresses a need or when a social worker has a client family that could benefit from actual family planning (that is how to run a family) a team could go to the home and assist them with developing a family routine to make their lives better and to facilitate putting families on a track of stability and self-reliance.

Tutor America

In the day of the Internet, it is not required that people be on site to tutor high school and college students. When referred to this service a student would receive help from a pool of online students and others who were good with schoolwork to help needy students with homework and school related activities. This service should be available to help with routine homework, to be a reminder for the students to stay caught up with homework and help with problem areas and with class projects.

International Commerce Start-Up Corp

This is intended for those people who are unemployed and on assistance who wish to venture to foreign lands but it would be open to any individual. It centers on helping build manufacturing facilities for native workers. They will own a majority of the facility and get a majority of the profits from the venture. Multinational companies may help pay for the construction of the facilities and for the equipment in exchange for partial ownership or may offer to contract for the goods and services to help establish the startup ventures.

Mobile Medical Corps

With the high cost of healthcare many go without seeing a doctor. Where there are concentrated areas of poor people, a mobile RV clinic could park in the streets of needy neighborhoods, plant locations or wherever most workers do not have insurance or access to medical care. It could also have an internet component for people to check online to receive medical services and information.

Urban Removal Land Rush

Some of the congestion in urban areas could be relieved by building new communities on outlying land where there are lower land values using the same formula for renewing housing with construction crews made up of unemployed and able body workers who are receiving public benefits.

50 New Cities

In a larger proposal, at some point America will need to move some of the population congestion away from the largest cities to new areas. Only the power of the federal government can plan and purchase large tracts of land in currently underutilized areas and layout completely new cities. These areas would need to be close to interstate highways and hopefully have natural attractions like mountains, lakes, etc. that will draw people away from the overcrowding of urban areas and to attract people from rural areas who wish to live in a place that is newly designed. Other considerations would be to locate near a water aquifer and near access to the power and utility grids.

The approach could be started with several test cities across the country and adding new ones when it seems prudent to do so. Some of the many advantages of having totally new and planned cities is that everything would be new, modern, and efficient.

Renew National Parks, Neighborhood Parks, and Build Sidewalks

Today we are stuck indoors too often. Not only are children playing more electronic games indoors but adults stay in the air conditioning during the heat of summer. Fewer of us are going out and meeting people and seeing one another. Gone too are the days of sitting on the front porch of homes and talking with people as they walk by. So that people can go outdoors and (1) get exercise and (2) meet their fellow citizens we should renew our efforts of building parks, particularly neighborhood ones, along walkways and bicycle paths for the same reasons.

Too much Government

Just a quick word to say that cameras at traffic intersections are just a bit too much government oversight. We don't want, as a free people, to be under surveillance and this is where we need to draw the line. Having video coverage of sidewalks for our mutual protection is one thing but we don't want to be under surveillance, not even when we are in our cars. It borders on oppression. That is my take on it anyway.

Part 4 - Planet Earth, Some Assembly Required

Chapter 19 - Being a Good World Partner

Despite all our modern development, inventions, and conveniences, human behavior has been the same since history was first recorded. There are good traits and bad traits in all of us and when pushed, trapped, or tempted, many of us can have human failings. Sometimes we even have a tendency toward it. As a people, we certainly are making progress with more civilized than ever before. The world is getting better. However, there are significant problems around the world as people separate themselves into different group identities and reject those who are different from them. We need to fight these defects. There seems to be a need in some emerging nations to purge anyone different from themselves, a tendency we have seen in America so we should be familiar with it.

The underdeveloped and rising nations can see us on their TV's, on the internet, on smartphones, and hear on radios about the outside world. This can be a powerful vehicle of change. It is what ultimately brought down the iron curtain. Before distant societies were so divided that they turned to conflict it might have been better to have sent food, clothing and offered to supply American know-how for their infrastructural needs. As we all recognize, America is good at water and sewer, housing, and utility development. If we do good basic things for people they are more likely to like us in their hearts and minds. That would be better in the long run than fearing us for our military might. It would cost about a tenth as much as we now spend.

When we consider the plight of the disadvantaged countries, we cannot say that we would like to help but that we don't have the resources. We have plenty of resources. We have enough financial resources as a people to do anything we can focus on. While some Americans complain about tax money being spent in foreign lands and hear examples of how it is being wasted most of us know that foreign aid is less than one percent of the overall budget. Other nations give more per capita, but it is not a major part of their budget either. Thankfully, there are countless humanitarian relief agencies that have made a big difference in the world.

America makes and sells more weapons than any other nation. We need to export peace and progress at least at the same pace as the tools of destruction. Currently Americans spend about twenty times more on war than on international aid. Our goals should be for human progress and humanitarianism and not so much political and military activity. For all the military action we do across the globe we should also commit to equal that in peaceful actions. We should take care of our neighbors because it is right and because it has a self-interest component also. Those of us who are lucky enough to be in civilized areas and be above the struggle will never be totally free or secure if turmoil exists in neighboring lands.

If America wants to be truly super with its powers we will need to make the case for peaceful solutions. In the future our weapons may not make much of a difference if the problem is not war. If anyone is going to resolve overseas problems, it will take trained and knowledgeable diplomats to offer workable solutions to divisive problems among the warring tribes of the world and in those areas where people cannot get along.

In places where force is being used to leverage commerce it must be stopped, not with force, but with language and with business moves of our own. We need to play the game well and not so crudely by using weapons. When we do intervene it must not be in the vein of a colonial power wishing to expand its dominance, but to help a neighbor rise to support itself and to develop a good and fair-trading relationship.

A good reason to address the problems beyond the shores of America is that it is the only way to save America from being irrelevant in the long term and it is a practical way to return America to a country of prosperity. America cannot have a minimum living wage of around $15.00 or more per hour while there are so many developing countries with billions of people who are willing to work for a few dollars per day. Their lot must be improved, if only to help us here at home. We would be like Russia with a great military but no practical tools to solve world problems or further human development other than war and turmoil.

The people in every country must have something to lose when civility is disturbed. The lack of an ability or opportunity to do anything about it may keep people down for a while, but eventually they will overcome oppression and demand a satisfactory life. When people can be busy obtaining the goods and services that make life better, they will have less interest in fighting.

We can help other countries with crop systems for internal use to feed their own people and so on. Plus as they develop commerce they will trade with those who helped them. Even if they didn't trade with us in the future we would have profited from building a good system and introducing good standards so they might not need humanitarian help in the future. The same is true for places in the Pacific Rim and in South America. We need to make friends and partners in these places. Good things will come from helping people rise out of poverty and hopelessness. Giving them a start into a better life and a hand up will benefit and stabilize the world, which is in turn good for America.

Today, we need to be progressive in taking care of our poor here in America to show those in the underdeveloped countries that embracing our way of life will help them as so many of them are poor. We should also encourage, and where we can do so legitimately, require other countries to adopt similar standards for their people. If we show improvement here at home the world will wonder at the concept of a civil democracy. Along with helping others with basic needs and introducing a system of building and engineering standards, we need to export our best community values and our respect for the minority voices among us. We need to require civility in return, civility in their land and in the way they interact with the rest of the world. However, we must act in a civil way also. In recent decades America has shown many shortcomings from failing to stop genocide in Africa, to invading the country of Iraq, and for having a one-sided policy toward Israel and Palestine among other failings. We must do better ourselves.

Poverty and Violence

In areas of the world human violence and aggression is one of the key obstacles in removing people from poverty, hunger, and despair. Military conflict interrupts normal living and upsets human norms and results in lost productivity. It is costly to those who must defend themselves from a possible spillover of violence into their countries and it is costly to assist those who flee from the conflict into other lands. Military action is about ten times more expensive than humanitarian aid, including applying long term solutions.

Without conflict it would be much less expensive to support relief agencies and help them reach the people that so desperately need it around the world. Without the conflict, governments might find it easier to approve funding for relief goals.

Poverty is a weapon of mass destruction. When America leaves a dire situation alone in the world it creates a vacuum that some party will come to either assist or exploit. Sometimes other countries have stepped in and as a result developed trading partners that they can trade with now and in the future. That is a good strategic move. Sometimes, however, we have left the situation alone and extremist and military groups have moved in and caused great harm to weak and downtrodden people and brought more problems to the world that civilized countries will have to eventually deal with.

America is very capable and, in concert with the rest of the civilized world, there are great opportunities abroad for progress. There are also good employment opportunities in doing these things. There is a need for skills ranging from engineers to plumbers to diplomats in places as far flung as Malaysia to South America among many others. The world has many needs and we may encounter many difficulties, some of which cannot be imagined until we try it. Technical advancements alone will not further human progress without also having social and cultural progress. We can begin by eliminating some of the harshest of economic disparities between nations so problems will be more manageable as we intertwine our interests with theirs..

Slums of the World

As people migrate away from rural areas and into cities looking for work, the numbers of people living in slums, shanty towns and informal settlements are skyrocketing. Some of the slums in the world are so big they are like cities. Currently, there are 200,000 of these communities across the world, according to the United Nations Report on Adequate Housing, that number is growing exponentially. Even before the economic crisis of 2008, about one third of all city dwellers live in slums, slums which will grow by one billion more people within the next twenty years. While 90 percent of the world's informal settlements are in developing nations -- such as India and Brazil -- they are a worldwide phenomenon and are in European capitals and largest American cities. They build whatever they can for their immediate needs and as time goes on the area grows into a mesh of unorganized huts and squalor. Working with the established relief agencies throughout the world would be a reasonable approach to attack these massive problems.

Perhaps cities and towns in America and in other developed nations can choose a slum or an impoverished area and adopt them the way we now adopt a highway to keep the debris alongside the road cleaned up. Citizens could even go there in the summers or at vacation time to build housing and infrastructure as well as provide food and other basics. Some industries might be established there, too. A one-percent tariff on all goods and services sold in international commerce would go a long way toward providing the funding needed to begin to remove slums and transition the residents into a more reasonable level of living. Another method to raise funds is to offer a tax break to individuals and companies that put money into a fund for the purpose of slum removal and efforts to eliminate poverty. If needed those special contributions could be directed to a specific area and that might urge donors to give more if they favor that place for some reason or another.

Hunger

While hunger has always been with us since ancient times there has been an increased interest in resolving hunger recently. Living in our country it is hard to imagine how many people on this planet are malnourished. Africa has the highest rates of hunger with almost one in four people thought to be undernourished. The most rapid progress has been recorded in south-east Asia where hunger has fallen from 31 percent in 1990 to an estimated 10 percent today. Overall, the vast majority of 800 million people who live in hunger live in developing countries. About fifteen percent of all people in the Third World are undernourished. That is an improvement from the early 1990's when roughly 25 percent of people in developing countries were undernourished. Although great strides have been made in world hunger, still one and eight people on this planet are suffering from severe malnutrition.

Children are the ones who fall into hunger the easiest and that causes them to suffer from growth problems and suffer from illness as well. About half of all the deaths of children are caused by malnutrition and one out of every six children are underweight. It appears that women fall victim to hunger more than men as women are more willing to sacrifice to provide for their children.

Until recently it was thought the problem with hunger is that the need for food exceeded the supply. However, most experts now agree that hunger does not come from lack of food, but from food distribution problems or from governmental policies. The world produces enough food now to feed the entire planet. If the world were vegetarian that would be even more so. The principal problem is the inability of the people to afford food, some farming problems, and human conflict where people are starving. A change in climate (global warming) accounts for hundreds of thousands of deaths each year.

About ten million people are starving or in poverty as the result of being refugees from the Iraq war and refugees from Somalia. While they may not be on any lists, a million people are refugees from the strife in Syria. Recently that figure is said to have grown significantly. This places a burden on humanitarian care providers that otherwise could be helping elsewhere.

Another problem involving world hunger is that the developed nations have traditionally had different views on how to solve the problem of poverty. Everyone wants to resolve emergency problems, but views have differed. Several of the major players in food relief want to bolster the economy while others saw this as problematic and wanted to teach the people within the countries to farm and grow enough food to feed the people within their own borders. Recently it appeared that this view is now gaining more ground and there is less resistance to it from those who sought free trade methods.

There are many fine organizations that have years of experience and local knowledge that, I presume, need only to be asked how more resources could be best used. If we put one fifth as much into peace as we do into war these problems would go away. This is particularly true if there was less armed conflict in the world. The United States could easily find the 39 billion dollars needed to stop world hunger in a budget of four trillion dollars. It is rumored that Russia spent over 150 billion to develop the Olympic venues, one billion dollars was spent on an America's Cup Regatta one year and as much was spent on European Formula One races and well over 30 billion dollars was spent on the Beijing Olympics Games in 2008. I am not suggesting that we cancel the Olympics nor curtail professional sports and other similar amusements, although I would make that trade. I am suggesting that the problem is not financially monumental. It is like planning to put a man on the moon, there is money available if we as a people want to make the effort. For a size comparison, America spends about $700 Billion on military each year and here in America about 50 billion is spent on food stamps for the needy in our own country.

In procuring funding, just as the poor among us here in America do not have a constituency, the poor in other lands certainly have no way to lobby for funds. While America is among the leaders in generosity much of the humanitarian aid is done privately. The government does not support humanitarian efforts in proportion to the size and power of the government or of our country. I suspect there would be political backlash if there were great increases in funding for humanitarian efforts unless it was tied to implementing permanent solutions to problems that recur routinely.

One bright spot in all this is that despite all the complaints about workers coming to America is that when immigrants make money they often send it back to their home country and that has helped alleviate the problems of both hunger and poverty there, perhaps more than all the governmental contributions of other countries combined.

In good measure, this book is advocating the development of a worldwide societal plan to resolve age old problems. We cannot merely give the poor a plate of food, an allotment of money, and condoms then assume the problems will go away. Nor can we hope to use our great military to crush resistance each time it pops up somewhere across the globe. In America, and in much of the world, the fastest way to raise people out of poverty is through raising the incomes of the people in industrious societies and helping to establish secure agrarian economies where farming is predominant.

Clean Water

While the problem of water scarcity is getting better, the lack of clean drinking water is one of the world's leading problems. People need clean water to drink and some of us are surprised to see it is a problem in parts of the world.

Over a billion people do not have access to safe drinking water with about a third of those people living in Africa. Millions of people worldwide die each year from waterborne illness. In many third-world countries, women walk barefoot on harsh terrain for hours each day to collect water for their families. Contaminated water is often collected that can lead to illness or death in gas cans weighing 40 pounds. They are strapped to their backs as they bear the weight of the water back home. Women spend so much time collecting water for their families they miss out on the opportunity to care for their young children. The cycle of poverty continues. African women are disproportionately burdened by scarcity of clean drinking water. In most African societies, women are seen as the collectors, managers, and guardians of water. They spend about sixty percent of the day collecting water. Children miss the opportunity to attend school because they are expected to go with their mother and to, like their mother, do the household chores and cooking. Poverty is directly related to the accessibility of clean drinking water. Without it, the chances of breaking out of the poverty trap are extremely slim. Great improvements have been made in these areas thanks to the many water charities who are working toward a goal of clean water for everyone on earth. One problem is these countries face a lack of industrial technology to make solutions sustainable. Additionally, tensions between local governments versus relief organizations impact the ability to successfully bring in money and aid-workers. Economically, there is a great divide in the income gaps of the urban and rural people which hinder the ability of the poor to gain access to clean water and clean water technologies. As a result many water projects ultimately fail and many projects are not monitored to assure that they continue to provide solutions.

There are three ways to obtain clean water. Purify the water that is being used now where the water is impure, dig new wells near their towns and villages where water is not readily available, and transport clean water to needy areas with small tanker trucks. Water projects are among the types of things that modern people are good at developing along with installing sewer systems and at introducing better farming methods. Philanthropist and well-established relief agencies are attending to much of the most fundamental needs of those in dire straits like attending to problems of AIDS, basic medicine and food supply and projects like water, but there are so many rural areas that more effort is needed.

Pollution and Disease

In rural areas in Africa and many other places around the globe there is a need for basic water and sewer infrastructure. They are discarding waste into the water system and the untreated sewage that flows near homes hosts a number of water-based diseases. We are all connected environmentally. Pollution is said to be the highest threat facing our world and the world of developing people. The average clean water well provides safe, clean drinking water to a village of 400 for 20 years. Drilling a well costs an average of $5,000. If that is the case it is indeed one we should look at, prioritize, and put solutions in place. Along with infrastructure there are many basic medical needs in these areas and plenty of opportunities for people to go overseas to service, train, and help others. There are plenty of private organizations that can take the lead in this, that either need more money, more workforce, or a more peaceful environment so they can treat the people who desperately need it.

Sewer Systems in Africa

About 90 percent of developing countries dump their sewage water directly into streams or lakes. Roughly 2.6 billion people lack any sanitation whatsoever. In much of Africa, people are drinking water that is contaminated with sewage water. Many South Africans are drinking sewage water and have been doing this for several decades from rivers contaminated by sewage overflows from shack settlements and municipal treatment works. In addition to the parasites and bacteria that live in the water making it unsafe to drink, it poisons the fish and nearby wildlife that many locals depend on for food. According to the U.N., for every dollar invested in sanitation, $8 is returned in reduced public health costs and lost productivity due to disease. The solution to this problem is more than building latrines or basic sewage systems. In India, when basic latrines were built in the 1980's many of the people turned them into goat sheds or storage areas because the people were used to open defecation and could not understand the concept of why any sewage system was necessary. To fix this worldwide it requires a restructuring of psychology for literally two and a half billion people, which in turn means giving basic education to the people in the developing world countries.

Pollution

When I was in high school there was a paper mill and a power plant about a mile from the school. The paper mill would occasionally give off an odor that smelled like rotten eggs and if the wind was blowing just right it would engulf the entire schoolyard. Some days the entire valley would smell like rotten eggs. The wife of one of the plant executives told me it smelled like money. Occasionally, we could look out the classroom windows and see a blanket of smog flakes from the big smokestack at the plant. It looked just like it was snowing. The employees at the plant would often buy older cars and trucks to drive to work as the emissions from the plant would ruin the finish on their good vehicles. If they ever considered what that pollution was doing to their children at the nearby schools they never said anything about it. I can only conclude the negative aspects of these facilities were deemed to be the price one pays for employment and electricity. Perhaps they expected the government to monitor the pollution and keep people safe. They didn't.

In the 1970's smog became a visible problem in some of America's major cities. There was an interest in moving toward cleaner air, water, and clean fuels. It also brought to the discussion that many large and small rivers in this country showed signs of industrial dumping of byproducts into the water. There was a general understanding that we should not damage the environment as if there is no tomorrow. The country was having a public discussion about industrial waste, trash, and over packaging of many of our consumer products. There was discussion on smokestack pollution and tailpipe pollution, but today these discussions have lessened.

Perhaps one of our recessions put people on their heels about cleaning up the environment; maybe it was a fear that it might add to the cost of doing business. Advocates for smaller governments with hands-off policies questioned the validity of the 'global warming ' issue. There was too, of course, a campaign by those vested interests who would be harmed if the country turned toward ecology. Unfortunately, the environment needs to be a consideration in any economy if we are to pass on a livable planet to future generations of people. It is local, national, and a worldwide concern.

Globally, pollution and human contamination affects over 100 million people, which is comparable to global diseases like malaria or HIV. Worldwide, several million people die from air pollution and related illnesses annually. More than 3.4 million people die each year from water, sanitation, and hygiene-related causes. This pollution ranges from drinking water to dangerous industrial chemicals left in our clothing. Despite the overwhelming amount of water on this planet, only 2.5% of the total water supply is freshwater and only a fraction of that is drinkable. Over one billion people worldwide lack access to safe and clean drinking water. Five thousand of those people die every day due to the dirty water that they have no choice but to drink. In China alone, 320 million people are without access to clean drinking water. There are two million premature deaths globally each year due to indoor and outdoor air pollution.

According to UNICEF, over one billion people defecate in the open. In Southern Asia, another 778 million people in the rural areas practice open defecation. Open defecation significantly compromises quality in nearby water bodies and creates disease.

The bodies of water near highly populated urban areas have the most contamination. This contamination is caused by waste dumped by individuals and by chemicals legally or illegally dumped by private companies.

The most obvious result of water pollution is that it kills the aquatic life that inhabits water-based ecosystems. Dead fish, birds, dolphins, and many other animals often wind up on beaches being killed by pollutants in their habitat. In addition, polluting bodies of water disrupt the natural food chain as well, often with lead and cadmium, which are eaten by tiny animals and plankton. Later, these animals are consumed by fish and shellfish, which are then eaten by other predators, and eventually humans. People can get diseases such as hepatitis by eating poisoned seafood. In either our ignorance or our carelessness we seem unable to stop this chain of events.

More people die from unsafe water each year than from all forms of violence, including wars. Unsafe water causes 4 billion cases of diarrhea each year, and results in 2.2 million deaths, mostly of children under five. This is the equivalent of 5,000 children dying each day. Clean water is easily available for many of us in the developed nations, but in many other areas of the world it is a precious commodity. Water is the most important of the necessities for survival, yet billions around the world are at risk drinking the only water available to them. It's terribly sad that even water, a prerequisite for living, is the cause for so much death worldwide.

Children are only 10% of the global population, but 40% of diseases affect them the most due to their less developed immune systems. More than 3 million children under age five die annually from environmental factors. This is unacceptable for the current technological and humanitarian capacity of the world's leading nations. America, the world's most powerful nation, as well as the United Nations, have the capacity to affect the quality of life for the rest of the world.

In my hometown in Georgia, few people will eat the fish that is caught in the local river as it is said to have PCBs from the operation of a medium-transformer plant that operated in the town for many years. It is widely rumored that countless fifty-five-gallon drums are buried on the plant property and one wonders if any of the drinking water is safe. Many towns may have the same concerns about old plants in their area. It's estimated that one and a half metric tons of nitrogen pollution are dumped into the Mississippi River which feeds into the Gulf of Mexico each year creating a "dead zone" in the Gulf in the summertime roughly the size of New Jersey. In addition to destroying the environment, it eradicates all the local commercial enterprises that would otherwise promote the local economy. This affects countless people on the coast who either suffer direct health consequences or the loss of financial support. It's not just the Gulf that is affected; the entire ocean has 14 billion pounds of garbage dumped into it annually, most of it is plastic products. This pollution leads to over one million seabirds and 100,000 sea mammals dying in the same time span.

Sanitation and drinking water investments have high rates of return: for every one dollar invested, there is a projected $3 to $4 in economic development in return. In addition, the economic impact due to the lack of water and sanitation in Africa results in about $28.4 billion or about 5% of GDP because of mortality and morbidity. Freshwater ecosystems provide more than $75 billion in goods and ecosystem services for people but are increasingly threatened by a host of water quality problems. Freshwater ecosystems, particularly marshes, provide water purification and the assimilation of wastes, valued at US$ 400 billion worldwide. With the economic potential from improving the water supply worldwide, and the result being a safer environment for billions of people, a clear choice of action should be taken to improve the quality for all of humanity.

There is a need to consider the environment in our manufacturing. In the manufacturing of clothing alone, leading brands have been tested and found to contain hazardous chemicals, some of which break down to form hormone-disrupting and potentially cancer-causing chemicals when released into waterways around the world. There are about 80 billion of these garments produced worldwide annually. Every person alive and even unborn children carry hundreds of manufactured chemicals in their bodies, including some that could be linked to the textile industry. The hazardous chemicals and toxins that we interact with in anything from our clothes to our food are causing people to suffer physical ailments and in some extreme cases, death. The international community can and should develop regulations and enforce them to ensure the safety of the human population around the world. In the future there will be a human crisis in the emerging nations if it is not addressed.

There will be one and a half billion people who will need clean sources of water in the next ten years. Another one and a half billion will not have access to modern energy. Another billion people who live in slums and in poor housing will not have clean water and sanitation. About the same number do not earn enough to lift them and their dependents above the poverty threshold, even given the standards of their own country. The people of the civilized world can address these issues, but it needs to become part of the world conversation and it will take human and financial resources to advertise a looming disaster.

CAFE Standards

I have written about this before and there are many people

more expert at conveying the world's dire need to curb pollution. Perhaps one day we will, again, be concerned about our ecology here in America. It could begin with true CAFÉ standards for automobiles. Today under several administrations car manufacturers have been able to swap 'credits' with the EV manufacturers (basically Tesla) so they could continue making large trucks and the overpowered cars. Tesla benefitted from this in the billions of dollars. The environment, not so much. And perhaps that is the true driving force behind car manufacturers developing their own electric vehicles. So maybe I was, and still am, impatient. Maybe it is slowly coming to be. I have a three-wheel reverse trike that can travel 45 miles at highway speeds at the cost of $1.09. The vehicle needs virtually no maintenance with batteries that will last for 20 years. So by comparison, the industry needs to catch up.

Motor Fuel Pollution

In Georgia, once the legislators were lobbied, the legislators enacted a tax for electric vehicles of $200.00 per year. It doesn't matter how much you drive the vehicle or how much it weighs. You do get to pay another $100.00 if your EV is registered to a corporation. So where I was paying $40.00 per year to drive my EV the new annual tag cost me $340.00. Before this tax Georgia was number two in the nation in EV sales. After the tax Georgia was not among the top state in EV sales. Let that be a lesson for all of us in changing the taxing structure. Also, at the time I was trying to commercialize my EV and after the tax change the investor interest diminished.

If we can tax electric vehicles to be sure they all are contributing to the road tax perhaps we can tax vehicles on how much they pollute. It could be done in the same manner by simply adding the tax to the tag fee. Vehicles with large motors and poor fuel economy would pay one amount and those that have better fuel economy would pay less. There has to be an incentive put in place to get buyers to choose more fuel-efficient vehicles. We know this by looking at the marketplace today and seeing the sales of large trucks and cars when everyone understands what is going on in the environment.

The other approach is simply not manufacturing polluting engines. Rather than these large ICE engines, it would be more workable to produce hybrids that had a small electric motor and battery set for short trips along with a small ICE engine with a maximum of around 125 HP for long trips. The electric motor could also kick in when short spurts of more horsepower were needed. People would have to get on board for such a shift because so many are addicted to having high output ICE power but it is the only way to stop the pollution that is causing illnesses and causing climate change.

What Would Happen if 'We' Do Nothing

So many Americans are content not to make any changes in their lives to help the environment. Men, in particular, seem to find it a necessary to have a big pick-up truck although they work at an insurance office. While they are having no worries just keep in mind that in as little as thirty years the temperatures could reach 120 to 140 degrees so plan to dress accordingly. Clean water will be for sale everywhere but few will be giving clean water away. The air will be dirty. A mask might do in some areas but in other areas a breathing device of some sort will be needed. That is if we do nothing. We are going a little now and hopefully, well, it's up to you.

Motor Fuel Costs

Few of us understand why motor fuel prices change on any given day and why the prices can vary among service stations in the same area. Long ago I studied this phenomenon and found it a bit complicated with the commodity market causing some of the fluctuation in the end pricing. I think more government participation could bring stability to that aspect and my other idea is to simply state a price norm year season and give the industry incentives to stay at the price. Say the standard price of regular gas is set at $2.99 for a given year. If the price goes down then nothing happens. If the price goes up there are disincentives such as higher taxes for the fuel provider on the fuel sold at a higher price. The reason the public is disenchanted with the system is that fuel producers are making record profits each year. In the insurance industry the individual insurance companies must ask a commissioner before they can increase rates. Perhaps the same approach may be needed for other parts of the economy.

Noise Pollution

Whether we are talking about established or developing nations, noise pollution is something that is sometimes overlooked. Some industries have noise making machinery that can run night and day. Some communities listen to a continental hum of noise and that they seemingly grow used to it. But they should not have to. Sometimes in our neighborhood, particularly where people live close together, residents play music or watch TV so loud it can be heard far beyond the walls of their dwelling. The same thing happens in cars. It is not unusual to hear the loud thump of a base speaker long before a vehicle pulls up next to us at a stop light. For those lucky enough to be in a marina at night, it is a rarity not to hear the loud music from a nearby boat. It is simply inconsiderate for others. As the population increases we will have to learn to be more considerate of our neighbors as we will be living closer together.

One International Standard

We should require all goods and services that come into this country to have been produced in an environment that lives up to a set of international OCHA standards to assure worker safety and clean working conditions that do not expose either the worker or the local environment to risks. An international standard of health for the global community would increase the average life expectancy and improve economic stability in countries around the world. Since no country is independent of another completely, an improved health and economic system in undeveloped countries is beneficial for all countries. Some standards like building codes and sewer standards may have to come in the form of recommendations, but we can add incentives and offer help to developing nations to improve their standards to safer levels.

Chapter 20 - Conflicts Around the Globe

Post October 7- America has an Israel Problem

In 1917, after intense lobbying from the Jewish community, Britain offered the Jewish people a national homeland in Palestine after the allied victory in World War I. The Jewish claim to that land was set out in the Balfour Declaration. It stated that it be "clearly understood that nothing shall be done which may prejudice the civil and religious rights of existing non-Jewish communities in Palestine." However, this was never given any notice then or today. Throughout the years, Israel has been strong, cunning, and aggressive. They are the best propagandist the world has ever known.

In the 1950's Israel stated they wanted to be a nation that can stand alone without the aid of any other country. This did not last long as Israel found they could do about anything with the support of the United States behind them. At first the United States wanted to use Israel as a military outpost in the Middle East. As early as 1968, Israel had secured continual support from Washington by systematically supporting candidates they liked and quietly opposing candidates they did not. They also underwrote trips to Israel for office holders, students, and others. They also enjoy the support of many in the Christian community as well has having supporters in high places in government, industry, and the media. To stand up against Israel has been thought political suicide for decades. They are in strong control within the establishment and among the American public.

In 2007 Jimmy Carter wrote a book critical of Israel pointing out their mistreatment of the Palestinians and he also spoke out about the power supporters of Israel have over congress. It has done little good.

Few Americans have stopped to realize the high costs for our blind support of Israel but in those costs would be the cost of the 1973 Oil Embargo which beforehand oil pricing had always favored America. Also, without our one-sided support of Israel there would not have been a 911 and no need for the security checks at airports.

As it turns out, the world needs to be careful when it gives away someone else's land. Britain and America had a big hand in upsetting that region of the world. The turmoil has disrupted human progress for one hundred years. It is time to acknowledge the error and produce an equitable solution.

The Best Laid Plan of Mice and Men: Russia Invades Ukraine

 As I try to convince the reader that war on a large scale is both politically and economically untenable in the 2022 edition of this book, Russian President Vladimir Putin invades the sovereign country of Ukraine. Initially my thought was how surreal and what that it was an unexpected move. The Invasion made little sense. But that is because most of us, including me, did not follow the events over there closely enough. There was a long build-up along the border of the two countries and military experts should have noticed this for what it was. We could have helped Ukraine more or at least had a plan on how to aid them more efficiently if and when the time came. Putin has been bold in his actions over the last ten or so years and has done things from assassinating a journalist in London in 2006 to his aggression in Syria and his annexation of Crimea among other things that he should have been called out on.

It is now known that he and his Russian military generals thought they could take all Ukraine within the first twelve hours. One might conclude they thought that Ukraine would roll over in view of the much stronger Russian army coming across their borders. That did not happen. Few could have known the strong reaction the leadership and the people of Ukraine would have and that they would take up arms and fight the Russian invaders house to house if need be. It is clear now that Ukraine will never be a Russian satellite state.

After the fact, experts have different viewpoints as to why Putin invaded. First, Ukraine was beginning to look more like the democratic countries that Putin was constantly in conflict with. That was probably a prime consideration in removing that type of government and culture adjoining the Russian border. Perhaps Putin considered that a modern Ukraine might cause democracy and free enterprise to appeal to Russians too.

To all this I would add one political factor in that it was predictable that this world disruption would extend into the United States. True enough that upsetting the world flow of oil would upset the financial markets, raise the price of motor fuels, and increase the level of inflation. Vladimir Putin always saw Donald Trump as a more favorable choice for Russian interests. Without inflation and the higher fuel prices where would the Trump movement be today in 2022 America? Does this economic turmoil boost a Trump comeback? The answer is yes. The Russians are chess players and all factors are considered in making such large-scale moves. I cannot point to any written or spoken link between the former president and Vladimir Putin, but they generally seem to say and do things that worked in concert with each other. Food for thought as I think that Vladimir Putin is totally focused on negating whatever America seeks to do in the world on general principle.

Because the people of Ukraine decided to fight, it changes how the people of the world must respond to the situation. We cannot and should not ignore it. Now that this is a shooting war, the developed world cannot address it on a diplomatic front alone but they must support the Ukrainian army and civilians fighting in the field. It requires and has received a two-prong response. Although there were moments of doubt, much of the world has responded by supporting the war effort by supplying armament but not always with what was needed nor as fast as the Ukrainians needed them. The only way at this writing to stave off the invaders is to supply Ukraine with all the weapons to match the Russians piece by piece until Putin realizes the war will be a stalemate at best for his Russian army. He must know that every time he escalates in either intensity or type of bombardment that the other nations of the world will see to it that Ukraine is able to match him. Only then will Putin be willing to sit down at any negotiation.

I suspect Putin will only back off his war effort when he feels pressure from Russian citizens. The Russian public receives political information from one TV station that is Russian sponsored. Russia does not allow Facebook, Twitter, and the other social media companies to operate within their borders. There must be a way found to reach the average Russian and talk to them too. As of 6/2022 most of the Russians still support the invasion as they are told that it is an effort to rid Ukraine of bad elements such as Nazis. Now we hear from military experts that they feel Putin will only look for a peaceful solution when Ukraine can attack Russian territory. That would be an escalation but I can only relay the facts that I have heard.

As of 6 2024, the war is ongoing. In the future it will be very difficult for one nation to invade another if the world will put in the checks and balances outlined in this book. Even Russia would not be able to survive if the world cut off all trade with them. That is the second part, a requirement for all nations to stand together when a cardinal rule has been broken. It is essential that the world set up trade where we all use a countries' resources but not to the degree that any one nation or all of them are solely reliant on that source. That is not true today.

When much of the world was trying not to use Russian oil it caused a shortage of oil on the open market. That caused the price of oil to go up worldwide. China and India, who have great needs, took advantage by buying Russian oil at depressed prices. This gave Putin funds to run Russia and at the same time hurt the remainder of the world with inflation. The world must plan better next time. Also, perhaps America will do better in world diplomacy. Putin had made it clear that he would not have a NATO member next to Russia and the US was pushing Ukraine toward that. Maybe it should not have been pushing so hard.

Connecting the People of the World

If this war has taught us anything it is that all citizens of the world need to be connected. Citizens from all countries must be free to communicate with one another and discuss our differences and share our opinions. This must be free from government censors and control. As difficult as this might be to implement in some countries we see that it is essential. Putin is isolated from the people of his country and the Russian people are isolated from the rest of the world so this allows Putin to do practically anything he would like. The people of Russia are accustomed to this and may even accept it and think of it as better in some ways but we must have a world in which we can talk citizen to citizen and we must have a world where leaders can feel the pressure from citizens if they do things outside the norm.

The invasion of Ukraine has disrupted the world, upsetting world economies, causing many deaths, and billions of dollars and destruction of property. In the short term the free world is being put to the test and must meet it militarily and must meet it diplomatically. However, we must learn from this. As I have said, put truth on the battlefield with any other enemy and the truth will be victorious. We are not there yet. But, as this book advocates, we must get there. We are still a fragmented world citizenry and this disconnect with the people of Russia brings to light the need for a worldwide link between all citizens of the world. We must ask and require our government and other governments across the world to make this possible.

Civil Unrest Inside a Country

There are times when a segment of the people inside a country violently disputes the governmental structure. Once civil war erupts, generally some organizations or representatives of other countries ask the parties to sit down and discuss their differences. If that fails, the world seems to give up. More should be done to settle these types of disputes and a system should be put in place to deal with them as they are likely to represent the types of problems that the civilized world will have to face in the future.

If warring parties would simply abide by the conventions already developed there might be much less conflict in the world. There are provisions under the Hague Conventions (kind of adjacent to the more familiar Geneva Conventions) that stipulate arbitration measures before conflicts break out. If the modern governments of the world would enforce these conventions perhaps the smaller governments would be more hesitant to fight until they at least attempt to settle differences. America would be the first country to step up as they do not have a good standing in this arena either.

When unrest reaches a certain level, the developed nations should step in and broker a peaceful solution. The nations should encourage using the arbitration system provided but if no agreement is possible the nations should force a national vote of the people to determine if they have confidence in their current government or its leaders. All people have the right to say how they would like to be governed and all governments today should work within modern guidelines and limitations. The primary question is whether a government is oppressing its people or is it repressing a fringe of citizens who are not justified in their rebellion. Rather than allowing the most forceful side to win, national referendums can resolve these types of questions.

The nations of the world could put together a universal set of procedures for intervening in these situations when they see mass violence. There are many internationally respected groups that could oversee an election. The international body could oversee a plebiscite with proposals from the sitting government, the rebels, from other nations, and any group of individuals that seem to have popular support.

If the sitting government has any pretension to legitimacy and wishes to work with other nations of the world it should allow the national referendum. All referendums should ask several pertinent questions that apply to the unrest and either support the current regime or vote 'no confidence' in the elected official and their policies. The proposals would have to also include an economic and social plan and offer peaceful solutions to stated problems. It might include a new constitutional framework and a budget for the next year or two to give the country some direction. Each proposal would be linked to a set of candidates with a short term as a provisional government. If people are dissatisfied with them, perhaps they would wait till the next elections rather than go into the streets with guns. If it goes well they can have a vote of confidence along with an option to extend the term. This eliminates the justification for human violence. If a provisional government cannot gain enough popularity to repeat an election victory, the people will have to keep voting until they come up with a system they can live with.

If a rejected government gets a vote of no confidence and it will not step aside, they conflict with all the other nations in the world and should be sanctioned until they allow a vote of confidence. We notice that these are always authoritarian governments and that people who understand and follow civil democracies have fewer problems. All countries should convert to civil democracies as soon as their people understand the delicate balance necessary to maintain peace in a more open society. In the day of modern communication, any remaining country that seeks to rule with a monarchy had better be sure the people are happy and content.

Torture

Torture is now out of the minds of most people but it was at the forefront during the George W. Bush administration. During the years after 911 the American government and later, to a lesser extent, under Barack Obama, the government approved some forms of torture and arranged for prisoners to be taken to other countries for interrogation. I understand these countries included, strangely enough, Libya and Syria. There is little to say about it. Either you think the ends justify the means or you do not. I do not. It is a blemish in American history that it was done. I see it as illegal and immoral. It hurts American interests and the interests of civility in the world. Credible sources report that it did not produce any significant information. It is natural that the people who did these things or authorized them will defend their actions. I am more interested in defending our values. We must follow the values we espouse. Even getting bad actors like Bin Laden was not worth lowering our standards of decency. American detractors used this as a recruiting tool and in addition to the inhumanity of it, common sense says if it is fair for us to do then that makes it alright for our enemies to torture people they capture. I, for one, do not want American soldiers or any of the independent contractors that are captured from time to time to be physically harmed in captivity. It is one more reason why critics could say America should not be the decisive player in regulating world affairs.

After America invaded Iraq and Afghanistan the number of terrorists multiplied by ten times. It is only because America has so much military and money that we are able to absorb all these failures. Think of what all the money spent could have done back at home and even overseas toward human progress. That we would torture combatants shows how lost we were as a nation.

Returning to International Rules of Engagement

Any thoughtful individual thinking about armed conflict would eventually wonder why there are no rules to limit the carnage and protect those who are not in the conflict. There are such a set of rules. The problem is that combatants are not going by them. The Hague Convention sets forth procedures for arbitration of conflicting issues among nations and provides for thirty-day time out periods to work on settlements and have a cooling off period. If all attempts fail, then a formal declaration is required to begin a war. Terrorist organizations often do not abide by these sorts of provisions, but they should as well as developed countries like the United States. The Hague Convention also specifies neutral zones, hospital zones, and safe zones where fighting is prohibited. Children are supposed to be protected from harm as well as mothers of young children. Enemy forces are not supposed to seize either land or property unless they provide compensation at the end of the conflict. Many countries are breaking these rules, including the United States. Israel has claimed land seized in the 1967 war. Citizens need only to pressure our governments to enforce these provisions. In America, like elsewhere, we would have to start at home. America uses its power in ways that benefit America's interests and the interests of aligned nations that otherwise would clearly be, well, wrong. This has been done to such a degree that America should lose its permanent nation status which is the ability to overrule most other nations in the world. This is nothing more than the continuation of the colonial system that has existed for centuries.

Empowering the UN and the International Court of Justice

The United Nations would be a more effective organization if the so called 'permanent members' did not have special status and the right to veto any measure. In conjunction with that, the international court of Justice needs to be able to enforce the decisions it makes, on those rare occasions when they feel emboldened enough to make them. They are timid because countries are free to ignore them and make them meaningless. The reality should be the opposite. The court should be able to notify the international monetary exchange and withhold all funds going into a country, all travel into and from the country should be stopped, as should all commerce. This would include the United States and the other major countries in the world.

Make Killing Unaffordable

Anytime innocent people are killed in conflicts there should be a fine paid to surviving family members. This includes, of course, any innocent people killed in reprisal attacks. This doesn't make it right nor does it make it even but it is a start and it might draw more attention to these tragedies as the dollar figures begin to add up. If combatants can't feel sympathy for the loss of life maybe they can relate to it in financial terms.

For example, in the October 7th attack in Israel the Palestinians would be liable for the 500 or so Israeli civilians killed in the attacks along with the destruction done to property. At one million dollars per person that would be 750 million dollars once property damage is included. If soldiers are to be included in this figure that will add another 500 million dollars for the IDF soldiers killed in the two encampments near the border on that day.

In the Israeli reprisals (as of May 2024) about 30,000 Palestinian civilians have been killed and about 50 to 70 billion dollars of property has been destroyed. So, in round numbers, about 100 billion dollars is owed to Palestine and Palestinians from the Israelis. America could be considered liable also as they gave them the munitions that did much of the carpet style bombing of civilian's residential and non-military structures.

Limiting Militaries and Armaments

One obvious way to extend peace is to make it more difficult to choose war as an option to resolve differences. Part of that would include limiting the size and capacity of a country's military to that of a defensive status. Japan is a good example of a country that is well defended within its borders but does not have or seek military powers that would enable it to attack other countries. At least that has been the case for many years. It has the assurance of its allies that they will help if needed. That would work in the future with other alliances. In the case of America with hundreds of military bases throughout the world they can be transitioned over to a multi-national force under NATO or the United Nations.

No nation should make money off the sale of arms. This is to reduce the interest in making them. No nation should export weapons to other countries without UN authorization and all countries should have just enough weapons to protect their country but not enough to start a war with other nations.

The countries of the world should eliminate most nuclear weapons, all chemical weapons, along with any weapon system that could be considered weapons of mass destruction. It would be a requirement of being a member of the world community and there would be inspections just like the current ones by the International Nuclear Regulatory Commission. In addition to agreements and having a 'most favored nations' status' for making such commitments we could add public pressure to the list of tools to help rid ourselves of the seeds of certain destruction. It would move us back to a time before Mutually Assured Destruction or 'MAD" as it was known. That worked when it was primarily the Soviets and the Americans, but it will not work with countries that have less concern for human life. We can't have that mindset controlling nuclear and WMDs.

There are enough landmines planted around the world (mostly in Africa, Afghanistan, and other war-torn areas) to be a problem for humanity for the next thousand years at the rate of current removal. As a people we must stop the mass production of so many weapons. We are getting too efficient at the production of weapons and they are falling into the hands of those who do not have the maturity to use them cautiously.

No Profits from Weapons

One way to cut into the over saturation of military weapons on this planet is take away the profits from those endeavors in addition to controlling the sales of all military weapons to only those sales approved by the United Nations for defensive purposes. No military equipment should be made for profit and no profit should be allowed. That should be a worldwide rule enforced with sanctions and tariffs. The same "Sunshine Laws' would apply to all the leaders in the defense industry.   7

Weapons of Mass Destruction

There are plenty of ways to end human existence on this planet and fewer ways to save it. If unchecked, continuing to have a nuclear armed world almost guarantees failure at some point in the future. First, and not the most salient aspect of reducing nuclear arms, is further reducing the stockpile of nuclear weapons. Second, we must freeze all nuclear weapon development. Next, we can lobby nuclear scientists worldwide to urge them to not work on nuclear weapon development and ask academics not to teach material that would lead to nuclear weapon development.

Russia and the United States have deactivated much of their massive nuclear arsenals but still much more needs to be done. It doesn't make sense to put the effort and resources into weapons that you see as being unusable in anything short of an end of the world scenario. Another round of SALT treaties is in order and they should include a total ban on all chemical and biological weapons as well as their development. Currently the U.S. and Russia have about 1,500 active nuclear weapons. That is both a danger and a waste of resources when a dozen nuclear weapons have the power to end all human life on this planet. Perhaps if nations had comparable conventional military powers they might give up their nuclear capability if their neighbors would give them up also. Reducing the number of everyone's nuclear weapons by ninety percent would be a good first step with 12 weapons being the maximum any one country can have. Countries that have a small number of weapons would have them reduced to one which would allow them to still be a nuclear power. This would allow them to keep both their neighbors and the superpowers in check.

The world cannot allow another level of nuclear expansion to develop into countries who find themselves in constant turmoil. One indication that a country is not mature enough for nuclear weapons is that they have little civil development and they are in near constant conflict. Unfair though it is to those rising nations, no further countries should obtain nuclear weapons as we seek to find ways to work back toward a saner world without them.

In an update since the COVID experience it must be added that in addition to a total ban on the development, manufacture, or possession of biological weapons that a worldwide committee also be charged to see that no viruses are developed or even studied in a way that may endanger the public health.

Soldiers are not Slaves nor Indentured Servants

In the modern world soldiers cannot be either a slave or indentured servant to the call of any leader the country might appoint. Soldiers are no more than prepared citizens and their lives are as valuable as anyone else's. We do not have the right to exert the kind of control over another human being to the extent that we compel them to kill people they do not know, for reasons they do not understand, or perhaps even support. In America, we were to have citizen soldiers. Soldiers nor citizens should never be forced into battle without full and free consent.

It is ridiculous that soldiers, who were often conscripted, must fight, and kill people they do not know, for reasons they do not understand or agree with. It must be all voluntary, not just the service, but whether to participate in a conflict. It is like a volunteer force taken from those trained in the military. This, too, must be the standard in every country.

America soldiers are being misused. They take an oath to defend our country but the military routinely uses them in many parts of the world where America is not in peril. Soldiers should be used for direct defense purposes only. If America wishes to be the policeman of the world the soldiers that do that should be there of their own volition. As a default, soldiers and citizens alike should advocate a conscientious objection to killing at any time unless they themselves or their homeland is being attacked.

Another example of the misuse of American soldiers is when citizens join the national guard in each state. The national guards are promoted as guardians of the homeland and to help in times of national disasters. I recently saw a National Guard advertisement to solicit new recruits on television. Again, they made it apparent the Guard was limited to homeland protection in their areas of their state and helping in times of natural disasters. However the reality is that many in the guard have found themselves serving overseas for a year at a time. The National Guard should only be used for defensive purposes at home and to help in their states in times of natural disasters. That is what the term "National Guard" means.

Compensation

It is sad when any soldier dies, but to make matters worse, their families do not receive adequate financial compensation in most of the countries of the world. In a matter of equity and to also cause war planners to consider the cost of losing soldiers more strongly, the families of soldiers should receive sums like that of people who are killed in mishaps in their homeland. In the United States, for example, that would be in the five-to-ten-million-dollar category

A System to Prevent War

Just like the world has a commission on nuclear energy, the world needs a commission to prevent war and conflict. It would monitor the level of conventional weapons, the sale of military arms within each country, and any sale of arms and munitions sold to other countries. It would monitor any buildup of arms along a nation's border and would figure the capabilities of all the nations' militaries and alarm all nations of any changes. If a nation were to become a threat to world stability it could trigger a vote to freeze that nation's money flow and to stop any material going into the country that might aid in violence or disruption.

The way to maintain stability and progress is to have nations strong and healthy but not so over powering in any strategic area to be able to withstand being cut off from the rest of the world. This was and is the problem with the current difficulties with Russia in their invasion of Ukraine. Preventing exports and imports does not work if the world needs their gas during winter. The secret is to benefit from their gas but not be so dependent that it cannot be done without for a short term of a year or two. This will be true of America also as America has shown in the past to be a bad player in world affairs.

Again, the relationship among countries must be that no one country is all powerful so that it could dictate terms to others and that no country is so weak it has nothing essential to offer the world. The world must work in an atmosphere in concert with the single goals of serving the humans that are on the planet as well as their own citizens. It must never entertain the idea of expansion of domination. Those days must be over.

When a bad actor comes along, whether it be an individual leader or a nation, the world must work to restrain that from happening by freezing goods and services into that country along with all travel. Seldom would that include food, but it might include energy. Withholding funds through the international money supply is probably the key to getting the attention of a rouge government along with citizen-to-citizen conversations when worldwide connections are made available.

A Policeman of the World?

As a superpower, America is somewhat special in that we are, apparently, the "policeman of the world." It would be a more perfect world if that role was, at least partially, shifted toward the United Nations where coalitions of countries could provide safety and freedom to those who need it. One major country attacking another should be seen as illegitimate, particularly when there is an absence of other countries joining them. Having large militaries allows countries to singularly invade others like Russia has done in Ukraine and like America did in Iraq. There must be an established and public need for such an invasion and supported by a multitude of nations, otherwise, it is just a large one nation invading a smaller one. Another problem that has been a problem for the world for fifty years is the one-sided support of Israel by the United States. Without that support perhaps Israel would have negotiated some sort of settlement by this time.

Again, money might be the answer. With international transactions going through an international exchange the exchange could without funds for a county who was being a bad actor on a vote by the UN, for example, or in the ways that we in some manner funds are withheld from middle eastern countries now. We need only ask ourselves do we trust other countries enough to join them as equals.

Toward Ending War

There is no single thing that will end all wars and conflicts, but removing poverty, hunger, and inequality among people would go a long way to make people less likely to want to go to war. Addressing these pressing problems might not guarantee peace but alleviating them will make the conflicts in the world more manageable. It would be hard to get fighters for wars if the people are enjoying improvement in their condition and where life for them and around them is getting dramatically better. We can't teach peace to people who do not have an education. Educating people in developing nations to read and write and other basic educational tools will enable them to see the diversity of the world in a better light.

Chapter 21 - Civility as a World Value

Cruelty is Repugnant

There is no place in the world for cruelty. Cruelty is the infliction of pain and suffering and it is also the indifference to pain and suffering. To be civilized we must stop cruelty wherever it exists. Where the modern world causes it, allows it, or tolerates it, it must end. When we stand by and allow harm to nonviolent and powerless people we are only one step above those doing the violence. We have broken our commitment to the treaty all individuals have with humanity and the world. They sat by and did not disturb us as we made our fortunes, but in places we did not hold up our end of the bargain by protecting them or helping them benefit in the societal structure. This would apply on the community level, the national level and on the world level. Everyone should have a basic opportunity for life, liberty, and the pursuit of happiness. In America, we have read that assurance all our lives. It is time to make it true at home and abroad.

Women's Rights around the World

Another issue that many in the modern world may not think about is the disparity between women's rights and men's rights in the global view. Perhaps many women in America would argue that they have not reached equality with men. They would point to the glass ceiling or to studies and anecdotal stories that show women do not get the same pay as men even if they are doing the same job. Studies show that, in fact, women are paid less than men in many areas of the American economy. While America has a way to go in achieving true equal rights, women in America are years ahead of women in other areas of the world like the Middle

East, parts of Africa, Latin America, and places where there is great poverty.

Many of the women in the Middle East do not recognize that they are discriminated against in the way we view it through the eyes of our western culture. Many women in the Middle East do not object to the traditions that basically subjugate them. I know personally that some of the women, for example, do not mind wearing clothing that covers their body and face while they are in public. They also see some of the traditions as being protective of women. While many in the west have the impression it is yet another issue with Islam, several of my friends say it is cultural not religious. They insist that it is the interpretation of the unwritten tribal laws and not the Qur'an that is the problem.

However, for all their support for traditional culture and their resentment of intrusion of western values, these women clearly suffer not only inequities but injustices. Sexual related injustices are occasional occurrences, but there are everyday inequalities and injustices that are a fact of life of women in that region. In much of that part of the world women cannot drive themselves or be seen in public without an escort, while problematic, they have real legal disadvantages as they cannot go to court without a male witness to verify that they have sufficient reason to be there. It is difficult to get a man to do this as they do not want to be seen as easing restrictions by helping the women. Women in the Middle East must have male guardianship and if for some reason she loses her husband she must have her son's permission to remarry. Women suffer greatly when looking at their well-being in a statistical view.

Women are being educated in much greater numbers in recent decades, but they still lag behind men in every area. It is a complicated issue but one where attention and focus must remain for progress to continue. In other parts of the world where inequality is related to poverty the answer is to remove poverty. That too has its difficulties. Resolving the world's problems is not for the impatient. Yet it must be done and without outside pressure progress would be much slower an occurrence.

Children Around the Globe

Many American families are pushed these days and wonder if they have the time and money to allow their children to join extracurricular activities that go on after school. This is quite a luxury from the standpoint of families of half the globe. They are so poor that their children must go to work to survive. While the world is making progress in human rights as of today there are about 85 million children who are put to work in hazardous jobs around the globe. The children are often chosen for jobs in the mining industry where they are forced to work to survive. In parts of India where poverty is widespread a family might give their children away because it is hard to feed them. Men from villages that might be hundreds of miles away pay a middleman to go to these villages and procure brides for them. The middleman keeps all the money, about $500.00. The parents look at it from the perspective that there is one less mouth to feed. These things highlight the great disparity in living conditions between the developed and undeveloped regions of the world. While the problems are so great that we may not expect a restructuring of society to resolve all problems, it is hoped that we can narrow the gap.

A primary goal of the world community should be to see that every child in the world has a chance to grow up in a home with food, clothes, an education, and a chance to succeed in life. Sometimes this might mean helping the parents obtain the skills needed to get a job and earn these things. Now UNICEF has such a program with this exact goal.

It is realistic to recognize that not all people are born into the same circumstances. Every person born deserves to have a happy childhood before they take on adult work. No child should go either hungry or unhealthy and no warrior should think their cause is so essential to endanger the lives of innocent children.

In the 1990's an American led embargo resulted in the deaths of hundreds of thousands of children. In such future occurrence these children should be sent food and basic supplies that could be taken in by relief agencies during temporary ceasefire or a ceasefire required through the insertion of a superior force of soldiers made up from the United Nations. Embargoes could be directed toward machinery, parts, industrial supplies etc. but not food for children.

People in Isolation

Earlier I talked about the requirement for all the world's citizens to be linked together, enabling us to talk about the issues of the day as a necessity and to have generic conversations as a nicety. Many countries limit communication in some way or another, or periodically, but there are countries that have forbidden open communications in total. Some countries have forms of government and culture that survive within their country but their leaders are fearful that citizens might wish for changes if they saw other possibilities and other ways of life. They also have concerns that open communications might lessen the hold they have over their people.

Foremost among them would be North Korea as it is a closed country. They are so removed from the modern world they, as I understand it, think their leader is a God. They are also taught that the United States is out to get them. They have never been exposed to what we would consider reality.

The great question is then, do we have an obligation to free their mind? If North Korea would give up all forms of offensive military capability as well as not harm the environment, then should we leave them alone? It is a hard decision. For now they show every sign of being an aggressor. If they insist on being a threat to the world then do we have a right to seek to undermine their leadership? I do think we could show the average North Korean pictures of the modern world and see if it interests them. Once they see what they could have it might spur some of them to talk among themselves about the outside world.

The Middle East has elements of a closed off society also. However, in the Middle East people like smart phones and enjoy the conveniences developed by the modern world. It is too late to keep people in those lands isolated as primitive religious states. That is why leaders use forceful means and that is why they limit information. They are on the losing end of this and since many within their borders want to change it is incumbent on the modern world to support and encourage bringing those people into the current century.

I would always remind people that, with a commitment to democracy and tolerance, that the international community will send food, erect housing, and offer education as well as security for them in their families. The extremists recruit among the poor and they also recruit along religious lines and with anti-American arguments. The messages must provide answers to those arguments and they should answer claims they make. Starting a dialogue is the first step in removing the battle from the streets and then into rooms where people can discuss them.

One thing we have learned is that, here in America, we get the establishment viewpoint in both domestic and foreign affairs. Skewed major media coverage of the 2023 and 2024 Israeli retaliation in Gaza has awakened many of us that there are two sides to most conflicts and that getting both sides of the story requires effort. We also have learned that money and power are at work world affairs. Not all of us are striving for universal human progress.

When rising people want to know more about progress, illiteracy prevents them from joining the internet era along with just having the time and access to a computer on the internet. Of course, one must be able to understand how to use a computer for discussions and to follow world news, etc. We all are challenged by that but it is the way of the future and having a connected planet. Once we secure the right for all people to be connected we then must be sure all citizens are able to communicate through reading and writing. Such improvements would surely have a positive effect on the world.

The Ethical Treatment of Animals

In my youth, there was no controversy on keeping animals in zoos or for institutions like SeaWorld to train dolphins and whales. Today much has changed but there are many ways in which animals could be treated better on this planet. One is centered on the diet of Americans and eating habits worldwide. For example, America slaughters about 98 million cows per year. I recall when I became a vegetarian about 50 years ago that people were sometimes unfamiliar with the concept and to the best of my memory, I had never heard to term 'vegan.' Today, of course, both terms are familiar to us as we see them routinely on restaurant menus. Also, there is a recent movement toward the concept of "plant-based" foods.

The diets of both Americans and others around the world have been centered around eating meat as a tradition. It is introduced to us at a young age and so we are socialized to accept this as the norm. When people try to give up eating meat they often find it too difficult to do.

Vegetarianism and veganism are trendy labels these days and the percentage of the population who practice them are hard to gauge. About 20 percent of the world's population are vegetarians, but much of this number includes those who cannot afford or do not have access to meat. In America the trend toward this healthier diet is reflected in the number of non-meat and dairy food choices but the figure for pure, consistent nonmeat eaters has always been around 2 to 6 percent of the US population. In England, the numbers vary with about 6 percent vegetarian, 3 percent vegan and about 6 percent who include fish in their diets.

While there are two sides to the discussion, research shows the consumption of meat is harder on the planet than plant-based diets. For example, the meat must be kept frozen from the time it is butchered. That takes energy as it goes down the logistics from slaughterhouse, to market, to home, and then to the stove.

Pragmatic arguments aside, the practice cruel and unnecessary in a world where we no longer need to kill animals to survive. However, it is a lot to ask people to change their diet preferences after being socialized to eat meat and their brains are programmed to want it.

I have noticed that it is impolite to mention how animals are slaughtered and in what quantities at the dinner table. People do not want to think about it. That should tell you something. Animals are a much higher form of life than plants. For vegetarians and vegans no animal has to die for them to eat a meal. This is an act of thoughtfulness.

I'm ready to move on to plant-based food. One day, our collective consciousness will need to extend to the protection of innocent animals from slaughter. When we live at that level of compassion then we will truly be on our way to paradise.

Chapter 22- One World, One People Connected

An Official Worldwide Feedback Website

Today, it is possible, practical, and desirable, for all the citizens to be linked to one another all over the world. A premium website could be more influential than any set of lobbyists, special interest PACs', media pundits, and government officials. It might be the one constant thing that might defray any attempt to sway the public with propaganda.

In the same vein as the official website proposal for America, it would link together all countries so citizens would be able to voice their opinion on public matters, tabulate preferences, and have a place for comments.

Citizens could react to any news stories. They could react to any new plans announced by their governments or events at home or abroad. Then they could list any grievances that a person might have with the government to see to see if others felt the same way. It would give a place for feedback on everything from government activity to media validity.

It could cover topics from gauging satisfaction with the government, work, community, and many other areas. It could forewarn of impending problems and be funded by the international community or in a way that no one government has control over it. Most of all, it could alert the world if people are being mistreated by their government.

Worldwide Survey

It would be possible to survey people all over the planet, and in time, each member of the planet. Some people would not wish to participate and fifteen percent of the world's population are still illiterate but many of these could be assisted by taking a survey. Still, because of technology, communicating with all the people of the world is promising. Surveys are a snapshot to how people feel at a given moment. Some surveys could be continually updated while others might be conducted several times a year or annually.

Direct Talking Before Fighting

No nation should go to war without knowing how all the citizens felt about being in war since it is their sons and daughters that will have to do the fighting and it is their country that will have the long-term brand of being in a war, particularly if they start one.

Not only could people voice an opinion that would be heard within their own country, but the people of each country could talk to one another. With people from both countries being able to all talk directly to one another it will create an interesting dynamic that has never happened in the history of the world. I hope, and count on, it making a difference.

Russia and Ukraine

One wonders, for example, if it would have made a difference if the people of Russia and the people of Ukraine could have had direct conversations before the Russian invasion of Ukraine. With citizens in direct contact with one another they could address issues and talk through accusations that are claimed in the media and said by officials on both sides.

Chapter 23- Permanent Solutions to World Problems

A New Renaissance

If we could start over is the current world format one we would choose for the inhabitants? We have a world where some countries are always at war or threatening wars, where religious and other differences are exploited to drive wedges in between people by extremists and often for manipulation. Most often the differences among people are exploited by those who wish to collect or maintain political power or financial wealth. At home and abroad we must weed out these issues that do nothing to promote human progress and certainly do nothing for peace and we need to weed out the people who use them for their personal enrichments or personal power. If humanity has a chance to reframe human organization, do it by leaving out as many things that divide people as possible.

Governments must act as responsible stewards of the planet and act in concert with other nations for the betterment of mankind. It may be the United Nations is the organization to do this or it may be a new one needs to be formed that does not allow a few founding and powerful members to veto anything they do not approve of. This caveat in the United Nations must one day be reckoned with.

War, for example, is a form of human violence so that is an unacceptable form of human behavior. Start with the premise that war is an unacceptable vehicle to resolve problems among nations and work together to force government to seek civilized solutions to those public problems among nations. We need a format in which to do this and a system among nations to enact progress. The system must be such that any government, country, or people can be isolated if they become bad actors in the world community. No one's power should be so strong as to be able to ignore the world community or to dictate to the world community. If we all trade with one another people in every country will want and need goods and services from other countries. With worldwide communications among all people we can all talk, text, and send videos to one another. That think that, too, is essential.

The day is over for powerful governments in general. Governments should make public functions work well, assure fairness and justice for their citizens, and enable fair commerce and trade. When a society has one set of rules for one group over another that is unacceptable in the modern world. There may very well be cultural differences, but we hope they will always be positive and progressive, but, like religion, they should be separate from the government.

If world governments cannot be moved toward human progress quickly enough, progressive people need not wait. Many things can be done without the government while at the same time pressing them to act. We need only find a way to identify each other. For example, we can develop our own network of communication as well as our own social groups and commercial cooperatives. We can develop fair trade among ourselves and develop 'Seals of Approval' on goods and services we find to be useful and of good quality and in our lives we should only make, buy, or sell items that are useful, of good quality, and priced fairly. We can continue to foster and expand relationships worldwide and push for a modern, progressive world. In doing this we must always be inclusive.

We want to reset the world where everyone has a safety net. A safety net to meet basic human needs as we all struggle to exist on a sliver of the planet. These needs include that of housing, food, clothing, and basic healthcare. Also, just as essential, is the need for a safety net to assure basic security, equality, and justice for all inhabitants. Any government that cannot provide these things should be on a watch list and then targeted with public and institutional pressure to meet these minimal needs. Again, one day we might have a worldwide constitution to assure us basic needs and general protections for all inhabitants. We want a worldwide middle class and have the economic system and political structures set up to protect and promote a vibrant middle class. We want the militaries of the world to be able to defend their homelands but not strong enough to be threats to other countries. We want to develop the necessary infrastructure like water, sewer, electricity, and other utility systems to serve the present and future needs of humanity.

Last, we want to be good stewards of the planet which includes treating animals with care. These are the standards that the current and future people will see as basic.

Specific Change

This book enumerates specific ideals, ideals, and proposals that would guide humanity toward human progress. Those based on need with America include:

Work Partnerships
Local Ownership with Large Corporations
Interest Rate Caps
Universal Healthcare
Access to Justice
No Tax Burden Based Student Loan Payoffs
Flat Rate Income Tax Structures
A New Candidate and Voting System
Building a One World Middle Class

In addition to the lists above, these are goals when looking at the global picture:

End poverty, hunger, and war worldwide
Reject any human violence
Work toward an immediate worldwide middle class
A worldwide communication system
Consumer protection and for workers' rights
Eliminate weapons of mass destruction
Reduce the size of militaries and armaments
All Armies are Voluntary
One World Connectivity
A one percent tariff to fight world poverty

Along with these assurances for the developed world we must weave into the fabric of rising nations some institutions that have been shown to be fundamental to having a lasting, peaceful, and growing society. Democracies seem to work best but they also require the people to understand how a democracy works, to know that it is a fragile system that can be broken if not maintained in intelligent ways. This requires the people under such governmental structures to be educated, not only to read and write, but to value peace and cooperation as well as being vigilant. Across the globe the various countries do not need to have identical constitutions, but they need to contain the elements of justice and equality for their people and offer both economic opportunities and personal freedoms. This should be required to be a member of the world community.

Conclusion - Toward World Peace and Human Progress

I hope there are people out there who find these proposals worthwhile. I do feel that the world we live in should more closely match the world we would wish for and more closely reflect the world we are technically capable of making if we had the human organization to make it so. If we want improvements, thoughtful and concerned people must unite in whatever ways are available within communities and across nations to overcome the barriers that are limiting the advancement of peace and human progress. If you want to change the system where our votes do not count for much, where political leaders are more attuned to the special interest that the interests of the citizens and the betterment of the society, then you must get involved. When individuals begin to advocate for ending poverty, hunger, war, and work toward building a vibrant worldwide middle class with equity and justice, we will be on the path to true human progress. What we do, individually and worldwide, is up to us. What kind of a world do we want to live in and how much effort are we willing to put into bringing it about? These are the questions conscientious people must ask themselves.

Among those who read books like this are people who can feel things, they are people who can imagine a better world, and they are people who might take small or big steps to bring it about if they have the opportunity. I think one would begin by living within the standards discussed in this book and advocating them to others. They would also seek out those who are like-minded. Being an advocate for peace and human progress is a strong and positive statement. Two people together would be twice as strong. A room full of like-minded people would make the foundations of a movement. I would ask you to make every effort to embrace the proposals in this book, live by them, promote them to others and be part of that movement to bring on the "Age of Civility."

Thank You, Jim Davis
Undated 2024